LIVING A SPIRITUALITY OF COMMUNION

To Chiara Lubich
founder of the Focolare Movement

Thomas J. Norris

Living a Spirituality of Communion

the columba press

First published in 2008 by
the columba press
55A Spruce Avenue, Stillorgan Industrial Park,
Blackrock, Co Dublin

Cover by Bill Bolger
Origination by The Columba Press
Printed by Athenaeum Press Ltd, Gateshead

ISBN 978 1 85607 610-4

Acknowledgements
The author is grateful to the editor of the *Irish Theological Quarterly* for
permission to republish 'On Revisiting *Dei Verburm*', 66 (2001), 315-338.

Contents

Abbreviations

Communio	International Catholic Review, Washington, D.C., 1974f.
DS	Denzinger-Schönmetzer, *Enchiridion Symbolorum, Definitionum et Declarationum in rebus fidei et morum*, Freiburg, 1965.
ITQ	*Irish Theological Quarterly*, Maynooth, 1906; 1951 new series.
PG	J. P. Migne, *Patrologia Graeca*, Paris, 1857-1866: 161 volumes.
PL	J. P. Migne, *Patrologia Latina*, Paris, 1844-1864: 217 volumes.
SC	*Sources chrétiennes*, edited by H. de Lubac and Jean Danielou, Paris.

Frontispiece

To make the church the home and the school of communion: that is the great challenge facing us in the millennium which is now beginning, if we wish to be faithful to God's plan and respond to the world's deepest yearnings.

But what does this mean in practice? Here, too, our thoughts could run immediately to the action to be undertaken, but that would not be the right impulse to follow. Before making practical plans, we need *to promote a spirituality of communion*, making it the guiding principle of education wherever individuals and Christians are formed, wherever ministers of the altar, consecrated persons, and pastoral workers are trained, wherever families and communities are being built up. *A spirituality of communion* indicates above all the heart's contemplation of the mystery of the Trinity dwelling in us, and whose light we must also be able to see shining on the faces of the brothers and sisters around us … Let us have no illusions: unless we follow this spiritual path, external structures of communion will serve very little purpose. They would become mechanisms without a soul, 'masks' of communion rather than its means of expression and growth.

Pope John Paul II,
Novo Millennio Ineunte:
Apostolic Letter for the Third Millennium,
paragraph 43

Introduction

There is a new stirring in the life of the church. A spirituality of communion is emerging. By 'spirituality' I mean a concrete way of realising or living out in the church the gospel revelation of the God of Jesus Christ. That gospel has inspired spiritualities of great depth and lasting fruitfulness, such as those of Benedict, Dominic, Francis, Ignatius, Teresa of Avila and Vincent de Paul, to name but a few. These spiritualities had, and continue to have, an impact on the life of the whole church, flowing as they do like streams of living water from the same fountainhead of the gospel. What is conspicuously absent, however, is a 'spirituality of communion' or unity.

What, precisely, is a 'spirituality of communion'? A contemporary authority in the field answers in these terms: 'In the history of Christian spirituality it was said: "Christ is in me, he lives in me," and that is the perspective of individual spirituality, life in Christ. When it also was said: "Christ is present in my brothers," this develops the perspective of works of charity, *but it falls short of saying that if Christ is in me and Christ is in you, then Christ in me loves Christ in you and vice versa ... which would involve a mutual giving and receiving.*'[1] In a spirituality of communion, one goes towards heaven not only with others but also *through* and *in others*. If God comes down to earth through his Son made flesh, then we

---

1. Chiara Lubich, *Essential Writings*, London 2007, 28 quoting a letter from Jesus Castellano OCD; italics added. This point is also made by Cardinal Montini (later Pope Paul VI), *Discorsi sulla Madonna e sui santi* (1955-1962), Milan 1965, 499-500, and by Karl Rahner, 'The Spirituality of the Church of the Future' in *Theological Investigations*, volume 20, New York 1981, 150-152.

ascend towards heaven through Jesus present in each sister and brother for whom he died. (1 Cor 8:11)

Now this absence is strange for many reasons. First, in St John's gospel, the summit of the New Testament's witness to divine revelation, the focus is on the very commandment that inspires communion through mutual love. (13:34-35; 15:12) This commandment Jesus calls both 'new' and 'his'. It is 'new' as expressive of the 'new creation' (2 Cor 5:17; Gal 6:15), that 'total newness Jesus brought by bringing himself who had been foretold.'[2] It is 'his' as essential to his mission from the Father. (Jn 10:1) Of it he says something that is not said of anything else in the whole of scripture: 'By this all will know that you are my disciples.' (13:35) Not only this, but at the zenith of his discourse at the supper in John, Jesus turns his command into prayer: 'May they all be one. As you, Father, are in me and I am in you, may they be completely one so that the world will believe you have sent me.' (17:21)

This absence is strange for a further reason. Together with the paschal mystery of the Lord's death and resurrection, the Blessed Trinity is the primary mystery of faith. Now the Trinity is a mystery of communion, communion between the co-eternal Persons in the Godhead. 'One of the Three' came to earth and became flesh of our flesh and bone of our bone. He came like a Divine Immigrant to bring the life of his Trinitarian homeland into history. 'In that day you will know that the Father is in me and I am in you and you are in me.' (Jn 14:20) On the night before he suffered he prayed: 'May they be so completely one that the world will believe you (Father) have sent me.' (Jn 17:21) Normally it is we who pray to the Father, but here the Son-made-flesh prays to the Father. In him we are One Person, (Gal 3:28) so that, as Augustine reminds us, 'If you see love, you see the Trinity.'[3]

The effects of failing to have a robust spirituality of communion or unity have been enormous. An Immanuel Kant could

---

2. St Irenaeus, *Against the Heresies*, IV, 34, 1.
3. St Augustine, *De Trinitate*, VIII, 8, 12.

write in the eighteenth century: 'The Trinity has got no relevance to practical living.'[4] In recent times, theologians of substance have contended that if the great doctrine were excised from the Creed it would make little or no difference to the spiritual lives of Christians![5] The mystery of the Holy Trinity has been individualised and privatised, being discovered within the life of each individual believer, *my* way to the Father! This led an Italian theologian to wonder whether the God of Christians is, in practice, truly Christian.[6] The most social of all revelations has become the most private of all spiritualities.

A further deleterious effect of failing to have a Trinitarian and communitarian spirituality was the increasing tension between the realms of religion and of everyday life. Faith and spirituality consisted in plunging into the mystery of the Trinity *as located in oneself.* However, the reality of one's concrete existence in the world included life with others. It included education and learning, work and industry, medicine and politics, business and communications, in a word, all that goes to constitute much of our human lives. These two blocks gradually separated and became remote from each other. Of this separation Pope Paul VI wrote in 1975: 'The separation of faith and culture is the greatest drama of our times.'[7]

The Lord, however, is the Lord of history. In the incarnation he even makes time become a dimension of divinity. He has promised to be with his church to the end of the ages. (Mt 28:18; Mk 16:16) 'The one who says this utters God's final decision, in that he himself is that decision: a definitive decision passed on the whole of history, never to be surpassed. It is a presence, which accompanies the church not only from above, as it were from out of the timeless world, but which submerges itself eucharistically in every moment of time.'[8] This 'eucharistic ac-

---

4. Immanuel Kant, *Il conflitto delle facolte*, Genoa 1953, 47.
5. It is enough to mention Hans Urs von Balthasar and Karl Rahner as examples.
6. Bruno Forte, *La Trinità*, Milano 1983, 11.
7 Pope Paul VI, Apostolic Exhortation *Evangelii Nuntiandi*, 20.
8. Hans Urs von Balthasar, *Elucidations*, I, London 1975, 75.

companiment' is perhaps the secret of the church's youthfulness by which she remembers the love of her youth when the paschal Christ made her his Bride.

That remembering, however, must inspire the church of the third millennium to venture 'new deeds' (Is 43:19) from out of the unspeakable riches of Christ (Eph 3:8). It is possible to trace that venture, as Vatican II dared to do. Following the biblical, liturgical, patristic and theological renewals of the first half of the last century, the Council opened up new vistas of under-standing. Taking its cue from the Fathers, it defined the church as 'a people made one from the unity of the Father, the Son and the Holy Spirit.'[9] The church is therefore a community modelled on, indeed participating in, the life of the blessed Trinity. Since this is the case, the Lord 'teaches that the fundamental law of human perfection, and consequently of the transformation of the world, is the new commandment of love.'[10] The theme of unity permeates the texts of the Councils, and is the key to the fourfold dialogue sketched out in constitution and decree.

Twenty years later the Special Synod of Bishops of 1985 ident-ified in communion the core category of the Council. When Pope John Paul II came to write his apostolic letter for the close of the Great Jubilee, he wrote these striking words: 'To make the church *the home and the school of communion:* that is the great chal-lenge facing us in the millennium which is now beginning, if we wish to be faithful to God's plan and respond to the world's deepest yearnings.' Having stated what is necessary, the pope warns against rushing into 'the action to be undertaken.' That would be a mistake.

Instead, 'we need *to promote a spirituality of communion.*' It must become the 'guiding principle' of all education at all levels in the church. In a word, since the church *is* a communion, her greatest need is to live by a spirituality of communion. As if to put his meaning beyond all doubt, the pope defines what he

9. *Lumen Gentium*, 4.
10. Pastoral Constitution on the Church in the Modern World, *Gaudium et spes*, 37.

means by a 'spirituality of communion'. It 'indicates above all the heart's contemplation of the mystery of the Trinity dwelling in us ... an ability to think of our brothers and sisters in faith within the profound unity of the Mystical Body, and therefore as "those who are part of me". Without this spiritual path, all external structures of communion can only become mechanisms without a soul, "masks" of communion rather than its means of expression and growth.'[11]

This volume wishes to outline some key moments in a spirituality of unity. Since this unity comes from the mystery of the Trinity, it will be a Trinitarian exposition.

The first chapter addresses the constitution on divine revelation of the Second Vatican Council, *Dei Verbum*. Its rhapsodic scriptural overture, drawn from the first verses of First John, is striking: 'We announce the eternal life that was with the Father and has appeared to us ... that our fellowship may be with the Father and with his Son, Jesus Christ.' (1 Jn 1:2, 3) The Council's categories are not only those of substance and nature but also those of relationship, participation and fellowship. The pulse of the Council can be felt in its conviction that if the world could hear the message of revelation, 'it would believe; by believing it would hope; and by hoping it would love.' The impact of the gift of revelation is such that it transforms the human substance to make it capable of 'trinitisation': individually and collectively the revealing Christ and the sanctifying Spirit draw us. They draw us upwards towards life in the company of the Blessed Trinity (Phil 3:14), a life beginning already now but offering the hope of a still greater fulfilment (1 Jn 3:2), indeed, 'the pledge of our inheritance' (Eph 1:13) while they push us outwards towards the deep sea of an authentic unity. In proportion as we realise this view of things, which we trust is the correct one, we will want to live worthy of the resulting vocation (Eph 4:1). A gospel 'art of loving' begins to peep out, inviting us to 'walk in love as Christ loved you, giving himself up in our place as a fragrant offering and a sacrifice to God.' (Eph 5:2)

---

11. Pope John Paul II, Apostolic Letter *Novo Millennio Ineunte*, 43.

This view of things can never be passed over as 'high theology.' Neither can it be left high and dry as a fresh understanding of an integrating mystery of faith *but without major repercussions for daily living.* On the contrary, it becomes an invitation to live the Christian life and so discover the 'life that is hidden with Christ in God.' (Col 3:3) Dogma has to translate into spirituality. Accordingly, the second chapter studies the new commandment, that commandment which the Johannine Jesus describes as both 'his' and 'new'. (Jn 13:34; 15:12) What is most striking is the principle of mutuality at its core: love *one another*! The 'new commandment' brings the life of the Trinity down to earth, for this is how the eternal Persons live *for* each other and *in* each other in the bosom of the Godhead. (Jn 1:18)

Aware, however, that, in the long history of the church, there has never been a spirituality of communion, one based that is on the mutual love shown in the revelation of Christ and specifically in living by the new commandment, this chapter offers an 'exegesis' of the new commandment, highlighting its meaning, its effects and its fruits. Finally, it underlines the eucharistic underpinnings of the commandment: for all of five chapters in St John's gospel, the Paschal Christ discourses on how to translate the commandment of mutual love into daily existence in the Christian community. It is one thing to receive the Holy Eucharist: it is another thing entirely to live by the sacrament that makes the many into one body, (1 Cor 10:17) coaxing them towards a new way of living for one another. (1 Cor 13:1-12)

What is the measure of the mutuality of the love? *As I have loved you.* (Jn 13:35; 15:12) Nothing less! Only when Christians perceive that Jesus delivered himself for us in a measure that is without measure (Jn 13:1) will they aspire to walk in love as Jesus loved them, giving himself up in their place as a fragrant offering and sacrifice to God. (Eph 5:1) Perhaps modern men and women find it more difficult than previous generations to find God in the vertical order: they first need to see him in the horizontal order. Karl Rahner rightly identifies in 'horizontalism' a summary of all heresies, a temptation to which post-ideo-

logical humankind is particularly prone.[12] However, the measure of love required to live by the new commandment is both
sourced in, and mirrored by, the Love that first loved us (1 Jn
4:19), and bled to death 'for us' and 'for our salvation'. This third
chapter sets out a selected sequence of moments in the history of
the church when some of Christ's greatest friends tried to respond to this love that first loved them. The result is a series of
'plunges' into the flow of the church's life across the ages. We
become aware of the vibrations of grace in history: is not history
the theatre where we experience the riches of revelation?

In the light of the understanding of revelation presented in
the opening chapter, and of the spirituality of communion unfolded in the subsequent chapters, must not Christians aim at a
new sociality? The fourth chapter sets out to suggest this new
'sociality of the gospel'. It cites an ongoing experiment in economics involving almost eight hundred businesses worldwide
and inspired by the charism of unity of the Focolare Movement
founded by Chiara Lubich. It begins with facts, not theories or
aspirations. The ongoing experiment, then, is proof that an
'economics of communion' is not only possible today, but imperative. Living it, Christians will be able to show Christ to the
world, Christ as a living Lord in their midst and in the middle of
economic activity. For as long as the Word of mutual love, 'the
pearl of the gospel,' (Pope John Paul II) remains only spiritual,
the Word has not yet become flesh in *our* society and for the life
of the world.

Such was the Christian revolution unleashed by the irruption
of personified divine Love, the Holy Spirit, at Pentecost that the
first Christians solved 'the social problem' overnight: 'None of
their members was ever in want.' (Acts 4:34) Can that have been
intended only for the beginning of the church, a kind of showing
of the authentic face of faith-life and Christian love-life, but confined to the beginnings? This view of church history has dominated for almost the duration of Christian history. But what about

12. Karl Rahner, *Theological Investigations*, vol 14, London 1976, 295-310.

'the simultaneously social, historical and interior character of Christianity'? (de Lubac)

The last chapter sets out to propose an ontology, an understanding of being that *seeks to reflect divine revelation, specifically, the revelation that at the core of Being there is communion, the ecstasy from self.*[13] If what remains in life and from life is not substance, as Aristotle claims, but love, as Jesus insists (Mt 25:30-45), is there not then a duty on believers to carry revealed insight into a responsible metaphysics? Since the Divine Persons are each identical with their relationships, must not relation come to the centre of this new ontology? This requires a revolution in our understanding of being. In the words of Walter Kasper, 'The ultimate and highest reality is not substance but relation ... The meaning of being is ... in self-communicating love.'[14]

The chapter begins with three primordial relationships – those of child to mother, of husband and wife, and to the other. A brief phenomenology of these relationships manifests the liveliness of being as consisting in loving. In fact, 'a thing is an identity in and through a manifold of manifestation or display or disclosure,' and 'each level of manifestation intensifies the identity of the thing.'[15] Being involves being-from-another, being-for-the-other and being-for-one-another. Exciting new categories begin to peep out, including relationality, reciprocity, mutual indwelling, self-emptying and unity. Above all, one realises with Chiara Lubich that 'the important thing in love is *to love*.'[16] These categories suggest some building blocks for a trinitarian ontology.

---

13. Henri de Lubac, *La Foi chrétienne*, Paris 1970, 13-14.
14. Walter Kasper, *The God of Jesus Christ*, London 1984, 156.
15. St Irenaeus, *Against the Heresies*, IV, 34.
16. Henri de Lubac, *Theology in History*, San Francisco 1996, 49; see n 4.

CHAPTER ONE

On Revisiting Dei Verbum

The Dogmatic Constitution on Divine Revelation of the Second
Vatican Council, *Dei Verbum*, enjoys special dignity as one of
only four constitutions appearing among the sixteen documents
promulgated by the Council.[1] This status is enhanced further by
the importance of the subject matter it deals with, as well as by
the recognised theological excellence of the exposition. *'Si jamais
il y eu un concile de réforme, c'était bien celui là'*, was how Karl
Barth evaluated the Council within a few years of the conclusion of the great event.[2] The almost four decades that have
elapsed since then have verified the assessment of the great
Swiss theologian. The Constitution, as the first formal statement
from an Ecumenical Council on the subject of divine revelation,
breaks new ground in many respects. This chapter will list these
breakthroughs, but only by way of introduction to its central
concern, which is in some elementary elaboration of motifs
often only hinted at in the text of *Dei Verbum*. In conclusion,
mention will be made of two seeming lacunae in the content of
the text. But first a word about the 'two languages' that seem to
be portrayed in the Constitution.

On reading Dei Verbum: *two Languages*
More than one author[3] has remarked on the fact that the text of

1. See Norman P. Tanner SJ, ed. *Decrees of the Ecumenical Councils*, vol II,
London and Washington DC, 1990, for the text of the Constitution in
Latin and English translation, 971-81: this will be our English translation except where otherwise indicated; for a forty-page bibliography,
see Gerald O'Collins SJ, Retrieving *Fundamental Theology. The Three
Styles of Contemporary Theology*, London 1993, 187-217.
2. Karl Barth, *Vatican II: La révélation divine*, Paris 1968, 522.
3. See Ghislain Lafont, 'La Constitution *Dei Verbum* et ses precedents
conciliares', in *Nouvelle Revue Théologique*, 110(1988), 58-73; Breandán

Dei Verbum speaks two different languages when one compares it with the preceding conciliar statements of Trent and Vatican I.

> The first language is *trinitarian* (revelation is distributed between the three divine Persons, each one having their own role, in other words, revelation as disclosed in the context of the 'Economic Trinity'), *communional* (revelation as directed towards the eschatological communion, but also as about a humanity shaped in a trinitarian way), *historical* (revelation described as a process which starts from the beginnings of creation right up to its accomplishment in Jesus Christ, and prolonged, in a certain sense, in its transmission, giving shape to Christian history).[4]

There is also a second language found in the constitution. It is a language stressing *creation/participation* (in relation to our dependency on God and to the autonomy of creation), *nature* (in relation to the divine nature as capable of being participated in), *truth* (in relation to the inalienable qualities of the contents of revelation), and *individual assent* to the God who reveals.

Which of the two languages has priority? There is a consensus that it is the trinitarian, with its stress on communion, that takes precedence over the metaphysical. It is enough to cite a passage such as the following to indicate this dominance in the tone of the text: 'In his goodness and wisdom, God chose to *reveal* himself and to make known to us the hidden purpose of his will (cf. Eph 1:9) by which through Christ, the Word made flesh, man has access to the Father in the Holy Spirit and comes to share in the divine nature (cf Eph 2:18; 2 Pet 1:4).'[5] One notices at once that the movement of divine revelation begins in the heart of God, reaches out towards the human heart, in order to draw

Leahy, 'Revelation and Faith', in Bede McGregor OP and Thomas Norris (eds), *Evangelizing for the Third Millennium. The Maynooth Conference on the New Catechism, May 1996*, Dublin 1997, 64-84.
4. Breandán Leahy, *op. cit.*, 65-66.
5. The English translation of *Dei Verbum* here is from the standard text of Walter M. Abbott SJ, *The Documents of Vatican II*, London and Dublin 1966.

men and women into a life-giving communion with God the holy Trinity and with one another.[6] *Cor ad cor loquitur.*

Ghislain Lafont notices that a whole new theological style emerged from the Council. That style is more communitarian in content and more dialogical in method than heretofore. It seems destined to exert an increasingly pervasive influence on all areas of the church's life, in worship, doctrine, theology, pastoral life, missionary life and inculturation. It is little surprise, then, that Pope John Paul II in his Apostolic Letter plotting the first steps of the church into the new millennium, *Novo Millennio Ineunte,* should stress that the most pressing pastoral goal of the church, the goal most in harmony with the Second Vatican Council, is 'to make the church *the home and the school of communion*: that is the great challenge facing us in the millennium which is now beginning, if we wish to be faithful to God's plan and respond to the world's deepest yearnings.'[7] If it is true – and Cardinal Newman contended that it is – that theology is the fundamental and regulating principle of the whole church system, then we have here a verification of Newman's insight in the fact of the new theology of *Dei Verbum* already setting the agenda and the 'style' for the church in the millennium now beginning.[8]

Naming the Key Breakthroughs
On the premise that theology is the fundamental and regulating principle of the whole church system, it has to follow that the various novelties mentioned, *or even barely hinted at,* in *Dei Verbum* are truly seminal for the future. And they are such not only for the area of revelation and fundamental theology, but also *for all areas* of the church's life and mission in the third millennium.

Among these breakthroughs the following are detectable in

---

6. See comments of Joseph Ratzinger, in Herbert Vorgrimler, *Commentary on the Documents of Vatican II,* vol II, New York 1969, 171f.
7. *Novo Millennio Ineunte,* 43.
8. John Henry Newman, *Preface to the Third Edition of the Via Media,* London 1891, xlvii. Paul Avis writes, 'If we knew where we were with revelation, everything else would fall into place', in his review of Gerald O'Collins, *op. cit.,* in *The Tablet,* 29 April 1995, 543.

Dei Verbum: revelation involves the interaction of 'deeds and words having an inner unity' (2); *the* deed which is also *the* word is the mystery of the Cross, for 'Jesus perfected revelation ... especially through his death and glorious resurrection' (4); third, the event of divine revelation is inseparable from the search for the meaning of life that constitutes a constant of the world's cultures, religions and philosophies, so that revelation necessarily involves an intersection between the human search for the Ground and the divine search for humankind (2); there is a renewed understanding of the relationship between philosophy and revelation; fifth, there is the role of the Holy Spirit in the economy of divine revelation as event and as gift, since 'Jesus perfected revelation ... through the final sending of the Holy Spirit' (2); and finally, there is the light shed by revelation as understood at the Council on the relationship between scripture, tradition and magisterium. Let us elaborate briefly on each of these themes.

I. 'DEEDS AND WORDS HAVING AN INNER UNITY'[9]

Dei Verbum speaks of 'the plan of salvation' being 'realised by deeds and words having an inner unity'.[10] Commentators have noted the sequence 'deeds and words'.[11] They stress 'that God reveals himself to mankind by deeds and words in close connection with one another; not simply by words, nor by words and deeds, but by deeds and words. There is a point in that order; the deeds come first, and the words interpreting the deeds come second.'[12]

---

9. Here we follow the translation of Walter M. Abbott SJ, *op. cit.*
10. *Dei Verbum*, n 3, '... *gestis verbisque intrinsice inter se connexis.*'
11. St John's gospel corroborates the same theology of revelation. Jesus' whole ministry is lived out under the pressure of 'the hour'. (2:4; 7:30; 8:30; 12:23, 27; 13:1; 17:1) All the events, from the first 'sign' of Cana, where 'He let his glory be seen' (2:11), to the great discourse culminating in the high priestly prayer, are measured in terms of their increasing proximity to 'the hour'. (12:23, 27; 13:1, 32; 17:5; 19:27)
12. B. C. Butler, 'The Vatican Council on Divine Revelation', in *The Clergy Review*, 150 (1965), 660.

The deeds, then, seem to have a certain priority. As in everyday life, the actions of a person speak louder than his words, so too in salvation history. 'The deeds wrought by God in the history of salvation manifest and confirm the teaching and reality signified by the words.' The words follow upon the deeds and their function is also vital, since 'they proclaim the deeds and clarify the mystery contained in them.'[13] This has a central hermeneutical importance. It shows why the single event of Cross and Resurrection is central to the New Testament whose inspired words then proclaim this multi-faceted event and clarify the mysteries contained in it. In some way, the very core of the Word to humankind then becomes the deed, indeed *this* Deed. One begins to understand St Paul's programmatic statement to the Corinthians: 'When I came to you, brethren, I did not come proclaiming the testimony of God in lofty words of wisdom. For I decided to know nothing among you except Jesus and him crucified.' (1 Cor 2:1-2, *RSV*) This Deed, where the eternal Word made flesh is silenced and becomes this Nonword, is the core of the Word![14]

God manifests and communicates himself in the history of salvation by a combination of deeds and words. This is true to the point that, as Cardinal Newman saw, 'Christianity is a history supernatural, and almost scenic: it tells us what its Author is, by telling us what he has done.'[15] This pattern of deed and word may be applied to the whole sweep of scripture. 'After this mighty voice (of God) had grown continually louder through the centuries up to John, the voice of one crying in the wilderness, it finally assumed human form and after a long succession of modulations of teachings and miracles which were to show us that of all frightful things that most frightful had to be chosen by love, namely, death, it gave out a great cry and died.'[16] This event and this cry lie at the core of the Word as finally revealed.

13. *Dei Verbum*, n 3.
14. H.U. von Balthasar, 'Centre of the Word in what is not a Word', *The Glory of the Lord*, Edinburgh 1989, vol VII, 77-89.
15. J. H. Newman, *Discussions and Arguments*, London 1872, 296.
16. Nicholas of Cusa, *Excitationes*, I, 3, as quoted in H. U. von Balthasar, *Man in History. A Theological Study*, London 1968, 282.

Not all, however, have been willing to accept the role of deed and word in divine revelation, and less still in that order. Gerald O'Collins mentions those who refuse 'to admit anything special about the events and experiences which constitute *Heilsgeschichte* or salvation history.'[17] These authors see little of intrinsic significance in these deeds and events, since '*Heilsgeschichte* and secular history are the same history: each from a different point of view is the story of God's providential government of the nations.'[18] The significance of the deeds lies in the word: without the word they would have no special or revelatory meaning. But this raises the still more urgent question: 'Why was this special prophetic and apostolic interpretation available for these historical experiences and events and not for those (of secular history)? Was there something about these historical experiences that both required and requires that theological reflection?'[19] If the greatest deed in the whole history of Israel is the total paschal event of the passion, cross and resurrection of Jesus of Nazareth who thereby becomes Christ and Lord (Acts 2:36), it is simply impossible to deny priority, and less still all significance, to the place of deeds and acts in the unfolding of revelation and salvation.[20]

II. 'JESUS COMPLETES THE WORK OF REVELATION ...
ABOVE ALL BY HIS DEATH'

In the neogothic College Chapel of St Patrick's College, Maynooth, there is a striking crucifixion in stained glass. In line with the well-documented medieval tradition in this field,[21] the Crucified Christ is depicted in a vivid trinitarian ensemble. The

---

17. *Fundamental Theology*, 75.
18. Stephen Neill, *The Interpretation of the New Testament 1861-1961*, London 1964, 264.
19. G. O'Collins SJ, *ibid.*, 75.
20. Of course, O'Collins is right to see the possible source of this rejection of the primatial role of deeds in divine revelation in 'their puzzlement about what could possibly be meant by "acts of God",' *ibid.*, 76f.
21 See Helen M. Roe, 'Illustrations of the Holy Trinity in Ireland', in *Journal of the Royal Society of Antiquaries of Ireland*, 109 (1979), 101-50.

artist portrays the Father holding the arms of the cross of his crucified Son, while the Holy Spirit in the form of a dove hovers between the Father and the crucified, no doubt as the sign of the emergence of the 'new creation' (2 Cor 5:17; Gal 6:15) from the chaos of the passion culminating in this shocking finale. The insight of our medieval forefathers has come back with vigour.

This return of a solidly trinitarian setting for the crucifixion of the eternal Son is an essential presupposition for the understanding of the cry of abandonment in Mark and Matthew. Both highlight the cry of abandonment as the one 'Word from the Cross' which Jesus speaks, *Eloi, Eloi,/Eli, Eli, lamma sabachtani. My God, my God, why have you forsaken me? (Mk 15:34; Mt 27:46)[22] The history of the exegesis of the text shows that, apart from the early centuries of the church, this text was almost invariably interpreted as Jesus praying Psalm 21 (22).[23] The consensus of contemporary exegesis reverses this view and sees in the text the revelation of Jesus' actual experience of his own death. Jesus is not for the psalm, rather the psalm is for Jesus (Balthasar, Moltmann). The sense of the cry, in other words, is to be determined from the identity of the one who pronounces it, and he is the Son who only on the previous evening had called God 'Abba' (Mk 14:36), having announced throughout his whole ministry the arrival into history of the God who is love and who comes to make a new history with us.

It is understandable that this violent and harsh event, this scandalous and shocking termination of the ministry of Jesus of Nazareth, could not but embarrass Christians from the beginning and throughout the ages. They are called, after all, to 'hear the Word of God with reverence' and to 'proclaim it confidently', as the very opening words of *Dei Verbum* stress. But what do

---

22. John does not refer to the forsakenness. However, one notices that his account of the passion is accompanied by references to Psalm 22 (21); see Ignace de la Potterie SJ, *The Hour of Jesus. The Passion and the Resurrection of Jesus according to John: Text and Spirit*, London 1989, *passim*.

23. Gérard Rossé, *The Cry of Jesus on the Cross. A Biblical and Theological Study*, New York 1990.

'reverence' and 'confidence' mean in this context? And Mark seems to go out of his way to highlight the dread and horror of the disciples as Jesus turns from Caesarea-Philippi (8:27-33) towards Jerusalem repeatedly forecasting his passion (Mk 9; 10). The Old Testament in fact carried the principle, 'One who has been hanged is accursed of God.' (Deut 21:23)

Since the end of World War II, theologians[24] began to take this moment of the passion of Jesus seriously and as a revelation of the truth the revealing Christ wishes to make known about the invisible Father. This cry of Jesus is directed towards the God whom Jesus had called 'Abba' only several hours earlier. It must therefore articulate an event occurring between the Father and the Son, though an event brought on by Jesus' executioners and, more precisely, by Jesus' own experience of his ultimate encounter with them as the one who has come 'to give his life as a ransom for many' (10:45). What is the content of the cry? Pope John Paul II answers in these daring words:

> One can say that these words are born at the level of that inseparable union of the Son with the Father, and are born because the Father 'laid upon him the iniquity of us all.' (Is 53:6) They also foreshadow the words of St Paul: 'For our sake the God made him to be sin who knew no sin' (2 Cor 5:21). Together with this horrible weight, encompassing the entire evil of turning away from God which is contained in sin, Christ, through the divine depth of his filial union with God, perceives in a humanly inexpressible way this suffering, which is the separation, the rejection by the Father, the estrangement from God. But precisely through his suffering he accomplishes the redemption, and can say as he breathes his last, 'It is finished.' (Jn 19: 29)[25]

Sinners are, by definition, without God, God-forsaken. The

---

24. G. K. Chesterton anticipates this new development in *The Everlasting Man*: 'For one annihilating instant an abyss that is not for our thoughts had opened even in the unity of the absolute; and God had been forsaken of God', New York 1955, 212.
25. Pope John Paul II, Apostolic Letter *Salvifici Doloris*, 18.

eternal Son coming on mission from the Father to bring them out of God-forsakenness and into communion with the Father (Eph 2:16-17), his 'Abba' (14:36), has loved them to the point of compromise. Because Jesus is God he is *agape*-love, but too much love makes him completely one with the beloved who are without his Father: he becomes God-forsaken with the God-forsaken. This outcome seems inevitable. He loses everything for love of his Abba *and* for love of us except love. Out of love for his Abba he wishes to give us his Abba as our Father, and has the appalling experience of experiencing him in that moment far from himself. 'O all you who pass by, look and see if there is any suffering like unto mine.' (Lam 1:12)

In Jesus crucified and forsaken one catches a glimpse of the kind of God who is operating in the passion. He is the God 'who to offer salvation to human beings, reaches them in their greatest distance from himself – whether it's the distance everyone is individually responsible for, or that caused by the personal and social malice of others. It's a distance which God has to experience himself, who, being Love, becomes one with us to the point of the cry on the cross.'[26] The extraordinary words of a document from the *International Theological Commission* immediately come to mind: 'No matter how great be the sinner's estrangement from God, it is not as deep as the sense of distance that the Son experiences *vis-à-vis* the Father in the kenotic emptying of himself (Phil 2:7), and in the anguish of "abandonment"(Mt 27:46).'[27] Thinking of this fact Hans Urs von Balthasar writes:

> We cannot emphasise strongly enough that this exegesis of God has no real analogue in the entire world of religion. Here God interprets his depths in suffering – that is, in a voluntary suffering, taking on himself the guilt of others; all the other ways travelled by man are such as entail the overcoming of

---

26. Giuseppe M. Zanghí, 'Towards a Theology of Jesus Forsaken', in *Being One*, 5 (1996), 56.
27. 'Select Questions in Christology', in *International Theological Commission*, 1979, S. 4, 8; see also Romano Guardini, *Der Herr*, Freiburg 1985, 475.

suffering, the quest for the 'happy life', or immunity to the reversals of life. All this is comprehensible. These are the typically human notions in which wisdom consists. But God's self-interpretation is in its foolishness 'wiser than human wisdom'. (1 Cor 1:25)[28]

What Mark brings out in his gospel, Paul has already highlighted in his letters. Paul rejoices to quote the Deuteronomic text we have already cited in his Letter to the Galatians.[29] However, he cites it with confidence, in fact, to highlight 'the revelation of the glory of God shining on the face of his Son'. (2 Cor 4:6) Both as a former rabbi and as an apostle, he is aware of the scandalous impact of the fact. Nowhere does this shine out more than in his letters to the Christians of Corinth, particularly the first. There he encounters two mindsets that dismiss as illogical 'the word of the Cross' (1 Cor 1:18) which for him is the core of the kerygma (1 Cor 2:2).[30]

'The Jews demand miracles and the Greeks look for wisdom.' Ernst Käsemann identifies here what he terms two 'egocentrisms.'[31] The first is the religious mode. It claims the right to determine in advance the manner in which God ought to show and reveal himself. Certain currents in the Judaism of Paul's milieu are of this clear mindset. In that way, they arrogate to themselves the role of measuring the validity of whatever God should propose. Such an egocentrism is simply closed to the divine initiative. It has already set boundaries to what God ought to do, or even could do, in his search for wayward and 'enslaved' (Phil 2:7) humankind. And as to 'the word of the cross', they are scandalised by the very thought. It is 'an obstacle they cannot get over'. (1 Cor 1:23)

---

28. 'God is his own Exegete', in *Communio*, 7 (1980), 284.
29. Gal 3:13.
30. See M. Hengel, *Crucifixion in the ancient World and the Folly of the Message of the Cross*, Philadephia 1977; *The Atonement: a Study of the Origins of the Doctrine of the New Testament*, London 1981.
31. E. Käsemann, 'Il valore salvifico della morte di Gesù in Paolo' in his *Prospettive paoline*, Brescia 1972; see also Piero Coda, *Evento pasquale, Trinità e storia*, Roma 1984, *passim*.

The second egocentrism is of a philosophical kind. Paul associates it with those whom he calls 'Greeks'. This is a philosophical egocentrism. It pretends to arrive at the final sense of existence and so also of the mystery of God with the sole energies of reason and speculation. God is to be found at the conclusion of a syllogism. In that way they arrogate to themselves the capacity and the right to measure the divine abyss with human intelligence. The intellect is the measure of the divine. From that perspective 'the word of the Cross' is simply madness (1 Cor 1:23).

Faced by these two egocentrisms, Paul proposes with formidable rhetoric and insight the crucified Christ as 'the power and the wisdom of God' (1 Cor 1:24). It is Jesus crucified and only he who is the true measure and revealer of who God is. Jesus crucified is the 'demystifier' – to use the word which 'the masters of suspicion' like Marx, Nietzsche and Freud applied to religion – of that attitude which would measure God by setting itself up as the norm of what is appropriate for God to do or even to be. Of course there is a way to approach God also from reason. Paul, in fact, champions that approach in Romans (1:20; 2:14-15, 17-18), as he had done while in Athens (Acts 17:23f).[32] Philosophy, however, is not capable of capturing 'the crucifixion of Christ' (1 Cor 1:17). Jesus crucified and forsaken challenges radically all philosophy and all other religion. As Pope John Paul writes in *Fides et Ratio*, 'Man cannot grasp how death could be the source of life and love; yet to reveal the mystery of his saving plan God has chosen precisely that which reason considers "foolishness" and a "scandal"(23).'

III. DIVINE REVELATION AS THE INTERSECTION OF SEARCHES

Gerald O'Collins notices that there are significant texts on revelation in the corpus of Vatican II outside of *Dei Verbum*.[33] A good case in point is the *Pastoral Constitution on the Church in the*

---

32. See Thomas Finan, 'The Desired of all Nations', in Thomas Finan and Vincent Twomey (eds), *Studies in Patristic Christology*, Dublin 1998, 1-22.
33. *Retrieving Fundamental Theology*, 63-78.

Modern World. In the former we read what has become an axiom in Catholic theology since the Council, 'Only in the mystery of the incarnate Word does the mystery of man take on light' (22). Pope John Paul returns to this text in *Fides et Ratio* and comments: 'Seen in any other terms, the mystery of personal existence remains an insoluble riddle. Where might the human being seek the answer to dramatic questions such as pain, the suffering of the innocent and death, if not in the light streaming from the mystery of Christ's passion, death and resurrection?' (12). Divine revelation reveals God to Man, and man to himself. Now this deserves a little unpacking in the interests of clarity.

The history of salvation witnesses two searches at the core of its drama. The first is the search of man for the ultimate origin or purpose of life. This search is identified in the 'the search from below', if that is the appropriate way to speak of it: '... all the nations might seek God and, by feeling their way towards him, succeed in finding him' (Acts 17:27). Cardinal Newman described this, as well as the religions that result, as 'the *Dispensation of Paganism*'. It is the

> vague and uncertain family of religious truths, originally from God, but sojourning without the sanction of miracle, or a definite home, as pilgrims up and down the world, and discernible and separable from the corrupt legends with which they are mixed.

It has to follow that there is

> nothing unreasonable in the notion that there may have been heathen poets and sages, or sibyls again, in a certain sense divinely illuminated, and organs through whom religious and moral truth was conveyed.[34]

Newman's thinking here is deeply indebted to the early philosophers and theologians of the church, especially those from Alexandria like Clement, Origen and Dionysius. They enabled him to understand that Dispensation of Paganism by

---

34. John Henry Newman, *The Arians of the Fourth Century*, 80-1, 82.

which 'nature was a parable: scripture was an allegory: pagan literature, philosophy, and mythology, properly understood, were but a preparation for the gospel. The Greek poets and sages were in a certain sense prophets.'[35] He came to understand that the God who is sought after in the plethora of pagan philosophers and myths does nothing in vain. It followed that 'when Providence would make a Revelation, he does not begin anew, but uses the existing system ... Thus the great characteristic of revelation is addition, substitution.'[36] Newman gives new currency to the Augustinian claim that God has given some revelation to devout pagans.[37]

Pope John Paul, in *Fides et Ratio*, stresses that

a cursory glance at ancient history shows clearly how in different parts of the world, with their different cultures, there arise at the same time the fundamental questions which pervade life: *Who am I? Where have I come from and where am I going? Why is there evil? What is there after this life?* These are the questions which we find in the sacred writings of Israel, as also in the Veda and the Avesta; we find them in the writings of Confucius and Lao-Tze, and in the preaching of Tirthankara and Buddha; they appear in the poetry of Homer and in the tragedies of Euripides and Sophocles, as they do in the philosophical writings of Plato and Aristotle (1).

To see the many texts of the ancient religions and philosophies as expressions of the search of humankind for answers to the 'fundamental questions pervading life is to point to the principle of intelligibility inherent in all these religions. The truth is that 'men look to the various religions for answers to those profound mysteries of the human condition which, today even as in olden times, deeply stir the human heart.'[38] Perhaps a little

---

35. *Idem.*, *Apologia pro vita sua*, London 1864, 27.
36. *Idem.*, *Essays Critical and Historical*, II, 194-5.
37. See St Augustine, *De peccatorum meritis et remissione*, II, xi, 16: PL, 44, col. 161; *De perfectione justitiae hominis*, xix, 42: PL, 44, col. 315; *De unico baptismo contra Petilianum*, I, 26-27: PL, 43, cols. 609-10.
38. *Nostra Aetate*, 1.

streamlining of the various answers may underline the nature of that search.

Here it may be helpful to speak in terms of different 'ways' opened up by the various religions. First, there is the Way of the primitive religions. At the heart of this way lies the search for communion with the more lasting parts of the cosmos. This search, however, has certain definite characteristics, including polytheism and mythology. There are the many 'gods' and each corresponds to basic needs such as the need for security, for protection, for fertility and so forth. These 'gods' are inevitably made in the image of the people who seek their patronage or specific blessing. This accounts for the anthropocentrism of this way. In mythology one reads the story of the struggle between good and evil, as for example in the Egyptian poem, The *Dispute of a man, who contemplates suicide, with his Soul*,[39] and the struggle between death and life, as in the *Epic of Gilgamesh*. In Ireland we have the extraordinary fact of the ancient neolithic tumulus of Newgrange which is a cry captured and frozen in stone of the human search for communion with the lasting parts of the cosmos.[40]

Next, there is the way of philosophy and of the great religions. In the millennium before the Christian era there is a special breakthrough in two forms, that of Greek philosophy and the great religions. This way places man's hope in reason as the tension towards the Ground of all reality, the Alpha. The greatness of this tradition is that it purified man's religious desire to seek the true God and pointed out the way to succeed in that seeking. There cannot be many 'gods', in fact only One and this One is not like any of the many things around us. To reach him, in fact, we have to tend towards him with seriousness of purpose and with the help of masters and the right spiritual technique. The search here ascends from below and requires the

---

39. For the text and commentary see Eric Voegelin, *Published Essays 1966-1985*, Louisiana 1990, 58-60; 66-68; 91-93.
40. See Brendan M. Purcell, *The Drama of Humanity*, Frankfurt am Main 1996, chapter two on 'Newgrange after the dawn of Humanity', 56-74.

negation of the self, the world and of things. All this means that the human, the starting point, is denied at the very outset. And the world and creation are denied: they cannot exist because the one exists!

The people of Israel, however, made a great discovery through the gracious kindness of Providence: it is not we who seek God, it is rather God who seeks us out (Deut 7:7-9). The history of Israel witnesses to this tremendous fact: the God of Abraham sought the deepest communion with the children of Abraham, and through them with the whole of humanity (Gen 12:3). 'When Israel was a child I loved him ... I led them with reins of kindness, with the leading strings of love ... They will have to go back to Egypt, Assyria must be their king.'(Hos 11:1, 4, 5). Israel knew in her bones that it was Yahweh who sought her out. However, her historic discovery was that she found it almost impossible to live in the great realm opened up over that time by exodus, repeated covenant, prophets and liturgy.[41] This revelation of deep-seated spiritual debility required a movement towards the future to an age to be ushered in by a Messiah and a Suffering Servant, as Second Isaiah stresses. The decisive weighting of Yahweh's design 'which stands for ever' (Ps 33:11) is transposed into the future. The fullness of Yahweh's gift is located beyond the present and can only be inaugurated at a time to be decided by Yahweh and through the agency of the Messiah and the mysterious Suffering Servant who, as Yahweh's comfort to his people (Is 40:1f), will 'do a new thing' (Is 43:19). The notion of the future time, the messianic time, is thus central in Israel. As a result, 'the pathos of Judaism is immense; it permeates all world history. Judaic expectations became secularised, not only in Marxism which forgets the basic covenant and acknowledges only prophetic movements, but also in the ideology of technical progress that fascinates all.'[42]

---

41. Hans Urs von Balthasar, *Herrlichkeit. Alter Bund*, Einsiedeln 1967, 383-4.
42. Hans Urs von Balthasar, 'Theology and Aesthetic', in *Communio* VIII, 1 (1981), 69. The author read this paper on the occasion of his receiving the honorary doctorate at the Catholic University of America in September 1980.

There are, then, the ways of the ancient religions, of the great religions, and of philosophy. These three begin from below and reach upwards towards the Answer. Then there is the way of Israel which is the way of Judaic futurism and hope. The first set is vertical in orientation, the way of Israel is descending and horizontal. It seems that these two simply cannot meet. However, 'what is irreconcilable in the world (the vertical and the horizontal) forms a cross, an empty cross that cannot be occupied by anyone. Jesus Christ alone can fill this empty space, because he is the fulfilment both of pagan human longing and of Jewish hopeful faith.'[43] Here the human search from below, in its many different modalities and incarnations in the history of religion and philosophy, effectively meets the divine descending search of Yahweh for Israel and humanity. The result is Christ who, according to the scriptures, is 'The Word made flesh.' In the striking words of T. S. Eliot, 'here the impossible union of spheres of existence is actual.'[44]

That intersection far exceeds the wildest imaginings of the human mind. Who could have ever imagined that the eternal Word himself should have left heaven and made himself one with a creature? (Phil 2:6-8). *Fides et Ratio* picks up the theme: 'In the incarnation of the Son of God we see forged the enduring and definitive synthesis which the human mind of itself could not even have imagined: the Eternal enters time, the Whole lies hidden in the part, God takes on a human face'(12).[45] As a result, 'participation in divine nature is not merely an aspiration, a continuation of the movement we experience within. Now it is a reality completed through the participation of transcendent divinity in human nature.'[46]

IV. REVELATION AND PHILOSOPHY

The approach we have adopted here in reading the texts has per-

---

43. *Ibid.*, 70.
44. T. S. Eliot, *The Four Quartets, Dry Salvages*, V.
45. See also John Paul II, *Tertio Millennio Adveniente*, 10.
46. David Walsh, *Guarded by Mystery. Meaning in a Postmodern Age*, Washington DC 1999, 93.

haps opened the way for a better understanding of the relationship between revelation and philosophy, and between faith and
reason. For our method follows both the order of history and the
order reached by specific differentiations of consciousness. It
follows, firstly, the order of history in suggesting the sequence
of primitive or compact cultures, the great religions, philosophy,
and Israel. In the compact cultures the divine, the human and
the cosmic are all consubstantial as it were. The great religions
distinguish the divine from all the rest as the first/last, the be-
yond/ground. The sequence concludes with the emergence of
philosophy in Greece and divine revelation in Israel. It follows,
secondly, the order of differentiations of consciousness which
seeks to understand this sequence as a set of definite noetic and
spiritual 'outbursts'. Man emerges as the one who in the whole
of the cosmos is aware of himself as a tension towards the
ground of all being (philosophy), while in Israel he discovers
himself as someone 'to whom the invisible God out of the abundance of his love speaks as to a friend (cf Ex 33:11).'[47] Israel
makes the collective and historical experience of being the one
addressed, called and approached by the very Ground of Being
who smiles on her as a parent smiles on a child.

The specificity and richness of the revelational differentiations now come into full view. In the Old Testament, God calls
and blesses Abraham, Isaac, Jacob, and their children for ever
(Gen 12:1-3; Is 6:8-13). Man is made in this God's image and likeness (Gen 1:26), Israel is the People of God, and the whole world
is his good creation. With the advance of this God's dialogue of
love with Israel (see Jer 31:3), a dialogue expressing his search
for the whole of humankind, there are new and astounding
'leaps in being'. The dialogue between this God and man becomes union when the Word becomes flesh, crossing the ontological abyss separating the infinite and the finite. The People of
Israel become the Body of Christ, and creation is resurrected
with the Risen Christ (Rom 8:22-5) to become 'the new creation'

---

47. *Dei Verbum*, 2.

(2 Cor 5:17; Gal 6:15). David Walsh puts the matter in these terms:

> The witness of Christ is not just a gain of intellectual clarity; it is the firm welding together of a structure that had only flimsily cohered up to that time and ever since. The most difficult and the deepest mystery of our existence now has definition. It is not eliminated nor even reduced, but its central structure is now confirmed. Confronted with the agonising problem of evil and suffering in existence, of the contradiction between the imperative of virtue and the persistent failure of achievement, we can be assured that their resolution has already taken place.[48]

In the earliest Christian times the unity of revelation, theology and philosophy was the norm. A vivid instance is Justin Martyr, a professional philosopher who became a Christian in the middle of the second century. The principal reason for his embracing the Christian faith was that he found in revelation not an alternative to philosophy but its genuine fulfilment. Christianity for Justin was 'the only true and profitable philosophy.'[49] According to Eric Voegelin, Justin is convinced that 'gospel and philosophy do not face the believer with a choice of alternatives, nor are they complementary aspects of truth which the thinker would have to weld into the complete truth; in his conception, the Logos of the gospel is rather the same Word of the same God as the *logos spermatikos* of philosophy, but at a later state of its manifestation in history.'[50] His view is typical for the early centuries.

It was precisely this unity that allowed the Fathers of the church to detect in the cultures of the nations the 'seeds of the Word'. This opened the way for an inculturation of the gospel that led to a new flowering of the culture being evangelised, as

---

48. David Walsh, *ibid.*, 92.
49. Justin Martyr, *Dialogue with Trypho*, 8,1.
50. Eric Voegelin, 'The Gospel and Culture', in *Published Essays 1966-1985*, Baton Rouge and London 1990, 173; see also T. Finan, *op. cit.*, n 3.

its particular *logoi spermatikoi* germinated in the encounter with revelation. Christ gathered up all the truths scattered up and down the world by introducing himself. However, he did so while also 'bringing a total newness by bringing himself',[51] as St Irenaeus stresses. This means that '[i]n practice ... one has to recognise, and make intelligible, the presence of Christ in a Babylonian hymn, or a Taoist speculation, or a Platonic dialogue'[52] while, *at the same time*, highlighting the arrival through the incarnation and the paschal mystery of the *omnis novitas*. This *novitas* in fact is 'the love (*agape*) of Christ which is beyond all knowing' (Eph 3:18). Even as it is communicated it becomes more mysterious.

A fascinating corroboration of this fact is to be found in the earliest Christian art. Original research shows that 'in its earliest beginnings Christian art arose out of the quest for the true philosophy', a fact that dashes the idea that the relationship between faith and philosophy is quite abstract. 'It was philosophy which enabled the first plastic expressions of the faith: ... the shepherd, the *orans* and the philosopher.' The philosopher image represents the true person of wisdom, the one who is the 'prototype of the *homo christianus* who has received the revelation of the true paradise through the gospel.' Besides, 'the figure of the philosopher now becomes the image of Christ himself.' For Christ alone has the answer to the universal problem of death. And the most penetrating question, the question piercing the side of each and every man and woman, is precisely the question of death. 'Philosophy, the search for meaning in the face of death, is now represented as the search for Christ': he is the 'one philosopher who gives an effectual answer by changing death and, therefore, changing life itself.'[53]

---

51. St Irenaeus, *Adversus Haereses*, as quoted by Hans Urs von Balthasar in *The Glory of the Lord, vol II*, Edinburgh 1984, 85.
52. Eric Voegelin, *ibid.*, 294.
53. J. Ratzinger, *The Nature and Mission of Theology*, San Francisco, 1995, 13-14.

V. 'JESUS PERFECTED REVELATION ... THROUGH THE FINAL SENDING
OF THE SPIRIT OF TRUTH'[54]

The place of the Holy Spirit in divine revelation is acknowl-
edged indeed. On no less than twenty-three occasions he is mentioned in the text of *Dei Verbum*. Still, his place is less substantial
than it might have been. The text is more Christocentric in content and, as such, is in line with the general tenor of Latin pneumatology.

Now this seems to be a great pity. Even a cursory glance at
the central events of the two Testaments is enough to highlight
the pervasive and determining role played by the Holy Spirit. In
the Old Testament 'he had spoken through the Prophets.'[55] It
was the same Holy Spirit who had brought about the incarnation of the eternal Word in Mary (Lk 1:35). And when Mary's
Son had risen from the dead and had shown that it was necessary (*dei*) for the Messiah to suffer and so enter his glory (Lk
24:26), he warned the disciples to stay in the city 'until he sent
down upon them what the Father has promised' (Lk 24:49),
namely, the Holy Spirit. Finally, Luke recounts the irruption of
the Holy Spirit when, at Pentecost, he floods the minds and
hearts of the disciples. He brings about in them the inhabitation
of the crucified and risen One, a kind of communitarian incarnation of Christ in a fashion analogous to his original, substantial
incarnation in Mary. This rapid and illustrative listing of the
'wonders of the Holy Spirit' is sufficient to highlight the relative
weakness of pneumatology in the text of *Dei Verbum*.

As *Dei Verbum* stresses, Christ the Lord is the one in whom
the full revelation of the supreme God is brought to completion
(cf 2 Cor 1:20; 3:16; 4:6). However, it is important to realise that

> the Spirit is not a second interpretation of God, but rather the
> perfection of the first and only interpretation, 'since he will
> not be speaking as from himself but will only say what he has

---

54. *Dei Verbum* 2, Abbott translation.
55. First Council of Constantinople, *The Creed*, in Norman P. Tanner SJ,
Decrees of the Ecumenical Councils, vol I, London and Georgetown 1990,
24.

learnt; and he will tell you of the things to come. He will glorify me, since all he tells you will be taken from what is mine.
Everything the Father has is mine; that is why I said: "All he
tells you will be taken from what is mine" (Jn 16:13-15).'[56]

In that way it is legitimate to see in the Holy Spirit the principle of reception of divine revelation.

While the Holy Spirit is not the 'second interpretation of
God' – 'it is the only Son who is nearest the Father's heart who
has made him known (*exegesato*)' (Jn 1:18) – he is the finisher and
polisher of divine revelation *with regard to us*. His is 'that divine
influence, which has the fullness of Christ's grace to purify us,
has also the power of Christ's blood to justify.'[57] Far from replac-
ing the Son made flesh 'who is in himself both the mediator and
the fullness of all revelation' (*Dei Verbum* 2), the Holy Spirit
serves to place him in human hearts and to enliven him in
human lives. A metaphor from the theatre suggests itself. Just as
the dramatic action on the stage tends to draw the spectators on
to the stage, so does the Holy Spirit manifest the action of the
Son to us the spectators who are then drawn into the action. That
is why the Holy Spirit is the key to revelation as a divine and
human drama.

An eminent orthodox bishop, Ignatios of Latakia, sums up
the matter with refreshing brevity. He wrote:

Without the Holy Spirit, God is far away,
> Christ stays in the past,
> the Gospel is a dead letter,
> the Church is simply an organisation,
> authority a matter of dominion,
> mission a matter of propaganda,
> the liturgy no more than an evocation,
> Christian living a slave morality.

---

56. Hans Urs von Balthasar, 'God is his own exegete', in *Communio*, XIII,
4 (1986), 285.
57. John Henry Newman, *Parochial and Plain Sermons*, V, London
1869, 140.

But in the Holy Spirit:
>   the cosmos is resurrected and groans with
>   birth-pangs of the Kingdom,
>   the risen Christ is there,
>   the Gospel is the power of life,
>   the Church shows forth the life of the Trinity,
>   authority is a liberating service,
>   mission is a Pentecost,
>   the liturgy is both memorial and anticipation,
>   human action is deified.[58]

In the earliest inculturation of the gospel outside of Palestine, that is, in the culture of Greece and Rome, there was at hand the understanding of logos, as we have seen in the case of Justin Martyr. The Greek culture provided an understanding of the human subject as logos, 'as the one in whom the absolute comes into expression as word ... In Greek culture we are confronted with the absolute and, through the logos, reflect on it.' It is easy to see why the first cultural area which divine Revelation penetrated was that which had made the logos its own. However, 'the categories of Greek culture did not allow for a reflection on the Spirit.'[59] The end result of this absence was that the role of the Holy Spirit, so powerfully highlighted in the very gospel that highlights both the incarnate Logos *and* the sheer centrality of 'the Spirit' who alone 'leads into the complete truth' and 'brings everything to mind' (Jn 16:13; 14:26), was not thought through. This failure easily led to the absolutisation of the subject as logos. This process has now reached a stage in European culture where the subject places himself over against the God of the incarnate Logos because that culture has not understood the truth that 'the human subject in Christ is invited to accomplish a

---

58. Metropolitan Ignatios of Latakia, Main Theme Address in *The Uppsala Report 1968* (Official Report of the Fourth Assembly of the World Council of Churches, Uppsala, July 4-20, 1968), Geneva 1969, 298; as quoted in Leon Joseph Suenens, *A New Pentecost?*, London 1975, 19-20.
59. Giuseppe M. Zanghí, 'A Reflection on Postmodernity', in *Being One*, 7 (1998), 81, 82.

journey in Christ.'[60] It is the Holy Spirit who shows the many directions of that journey and the *Lebensraum* which it opens for each person, for society and for the whole of human history.

VI. REVELATION IN SCRIPTURE, TRADITION AND MAGISTERIUM

Perhaps one of the most significant breakthroughs of the conciliar text consists in its going beyond the post-Tridentine polemic between the Catholic Church and the Reformers with respect to the 'sources of revelation'. That polemic involved the conflict between the Protestant *sola scriptura* and *sola fides*, on the one hand, and the Catholic combination of scripture, tradition and magisterium, on the other. On the Catholic side, the language of 'sources of revelation' gained the ascendancy.

Underlying this gigantic struggle was an understanding of scripture that was somewhat naïve and reductionist. The scriptures are not merely a written, albeit inspired, norm for the church's faith. They are much more than this. Besides, '*Scripture alone* was a principle that allowed revelation to be measured by the recipient, and not by the revealer.'[61] Tradition for its part is more than the living collection of oral teaching set in the living context of the church's liturgical life and abiding task of catechising for initiation and nurturing in the faith. It is so rich and subtle and varied that it will manifest itself in many channels at the prompting of the Holy Spirit and in harmony with the historical and cultural needs of the church on her pilgrimage through history.[62]

One of the glories of *Dei Verbum* is its vivid awareness of the need to go beyond the unsatisfactory formulations forged in the context of Counter-Reformation theology. Chapter two of the *Constitution* is clearly preoccupied with the effort to produce definitions of scripture, tradition and magisterium as functions of divine revelation and 'of the one sacred deposit of the word of

---

60. *Ibid.*, 82.
61. H. D. Weidner, Introduction to John Henry Newman's, *The Via Media of the Anglican Church*, Oxford 1990, xxxiv.
62. See John Henry Newman, *On Consulting the Faithful in Matters of Doctrine*, in J. Guitton, *The Church and the Laity*, New York 1964, 73.

God, which is committed to the church' (*Dei Verbum*, 10). The Council defines sacred scripture as 'the word of God inasmuch as it is consigned to writing under the inspiration of the divine Spirit.' It continues in the next breath, 'To the successors of the apostles, sacred tradition hands on in its full purity God's word, which was entrusted to the apostles by Christ the Lord and the Holy Spirit' (*Dei Verbum*, 9). Since the rubric, 'the word of God' is a synonym for divine revelation in *Dei Verbum*, one may see here the concern of the Council fathers to define scripture and tradition in a way that was more patristic, more catholic and more historical, and, by the same token, less polemical. In this perspective, scripture, tradition and magisterium are not primarily sources of divine revelation but its very media, its carriers.

The debate at the Council was much concerned to arrive at a more theologically accurate description of these media of divine revelation. An outstanding and insightful contribution to that debate was made, shortly before the promulgation of *Dei Verbum*, by the Melkite archbishop, Neophytos Edelby.[63] The archbishop concentrates on certain key elements in the total process of the transmission of revelation. As a first principle, 'one cannot separate the mission of the Holy Spirit from the mission of the incarnate Word' in the interpretation of scripture. This means, second, that scripture 'is the witness of the Holy Spirit to Christ' and being such a witness demands that scripture be seen as a prophetic and liturgical witness to Christ. 'Through this witness of the Holy Spirit, the saving plan ('economy') of the Word reveals the Father', and scripture becomes a 'certain consecration of salvation history.' It must follow that the Holy Spirit bends down over the deeds constituting salvation history and renders these deeds contemporaneous with the church in all her ages.

---

63. See *Acta Synodalia Sacrosancti Concilii Oecumenici Vaticani Secundi*, vol 3, part 3, Vatican 1974, 306-8. The text is available in English translation in G. O'Collins SJ, *Retrieving Fundamental Theology*, London 1993, 174-7; see Thomas J. McGovern, 'The Edelby Intervention at Vatican II', in *ITQ*, 64 (1999), 245-60.

This means that the Holy Spirit is an *epiclesis* over salvation history. Such an epiclesis renders the events of that history alive and present. This throws up the idea of tradition and the fact of tradition. In that way the Holy Spirit bears witness to the total event of Jesus Christ 'who is in himself both the mediator and the fullness of all revelation.' (2) The Holy Spirit witnesses to it in the pages of scripture and keeps it alive in the manifold channels and manifestations of tradition. This understanding of *Dei Verbum* allows for a much more vivid and theological grasp of the place of scripture and tradition in the total divine economy of revelation. That revelation is incomplete without its embodiment and expression in these media,[64] which are intelligible only in the light of the mission of the Holy Spirit and the mission of the Eternal Word. And what of the magisterium? The same principle of the double mission obtains, for 'the Spirit is the Spirit of the body of Christ. Tradition, therefore, should be regarded and lived above all *in the light of the sacrament of apostolicity – that is to say, the episcopate.'*[65] This grounds the teaching task of the successors of Peter and the Twelve.

Two Lacunae

In the light of such a fine articulation of divine revelation, which, in the words of Cardinal Newman, is 'the initial and essential idea of Christianity',[66] *Dei Verbum* can be seen to deserve richly the accolade accorded to it by Karl Barth. However, the text overlooks two areas that seem to be eminently deserving of at least a mention. The first of these areas is the need to employ the transcendental of 'beauty' and not only those of 'truth' and 'goodness'. Secondly, there is the necessity of approaching reality with trinitarian eyes. This requires the elaboration of a trinitarian ontology. Such an ontology would highlight the originality of revelation. In stressing the centrality of the Trinitarian mystery,

---

64. See Karl Rahner, *Divine Inspiration*, Freiburg 1966, *passim*.
65. G. O'Collins SJ, *ibid.*, 176.
66. J. H. Newman, *Preface to the Third Edition of the Via Media*, London 1877, xlvii.

it opens up the various colours of reality, what the tradition calls the transcendentals of being: it will not be enough to employ exclusively the categories of the true and the good. In highlighting the originality of the ontology implicit in revelation, it could have pre-empted the tendency of modern culture not to look to the gospel for inspiration or even dialogue. These areas can be associated, respectively, with the names of Hans Urs von Balthasar and Klaus Hemmerle.

a. Revelation as Theological Aesthetics, Drama, and Logic: von Balthasar

The thrust of *Dei Verbum* is such that a number of definitions of divine revelation either stand out or else insinuate themselves. Thus, revelation is the communication of 'the truth, both about God and about the salvation of humankind' (2). This notion of revelation adopts the category of truth, and enjoys a certain ascendancy in the history of theology. Divine revelation provides the great truths of the faith, its principles. This language of divine revelation as truth is prominent in *Dei Verbum* (see 5; and 6, 'truths'). The language of the 'good' is also there or implied. 'God is with us to deliver us from the darkness of sin and death, and to raise us up to eternal life' (4). What is absent, however, is the language of beauty, or its revealed equivalent, glory.

Now this is a glaring omission. From beginning to end the scriptures of both Testaments are shot through with the language of *kabhod* and *doxa* (glory).[67] From the heights of Sinai where God lets all his glory pass by Moses (Ex 34), through the call of Isaiah (Is 6) to the incarnation of the Son in the flesh of Mary (Jn 1:14), revelation has as its sustaining and expanding content the manifestation of the glory of the God of Moses, the prophets and of Jesus Christ. 'We saw his glory, the glory that is his as the only Son of the Father, full of grace and of truth' (Jn 1:14). God shows himself as beauty in the face of his crucified

---

67. See Z. Alszegy and M. Flick, 'Gloria Dei', in *Gregorianum*, 36 (1955), 361-90.

and risen Son, and interprets that face to us by the Holy Spirit (see 2 Cor 4:6).

Christian revelation is something that is done by God showing us Christ. He who used to be 'in the form of God' (Phil 2:6) appears in Christ on the stage of the world in the form of man in 'the condition of a slave', and in the golden words of St Augustine, 'turning us slaves into children by being born from you, Father, and by serving you.'[68] The root of this showing is in the ever-greater love of the Trinity (see Eph 3:19). Christ is the *Gestalt* of God, a word that has affinities with Hopkins' notion of 'inscape'. It means that Christ is the 'form', 'figure', 'shape' of God. He is the Father's consubstantial self-portrait. The idea may be clarified with the help of an analogy borrowed from the world of painting.

> In Christian Faith the captivating force (the 'subjective evidence') of the artwork which is Christ takes hold of our imaginative powers; we enter into the 'painterly world' which this discloses and, entranced by what we see, we come to contemplate the glory or sovereign love of God in Christ (the 'objective evidence') as manifested in the concrete events of his life, death and resurrection. So entering his glory we become absorbed by it, but this very absorption sends us out into the world in sacrificial love like that of Jesus.[69]

Von Balthasar has dedicated two of the six volumes of the *Theological Aesthetics* to representatives of the two Christian millennia who elaborated epoch-making theologies by perceiving the revealed glory of trinitarian, crucified and glorified love. The constant factor in all these theologies is the perception of Christian revelation as the inbreaking of divine glory into human history. The God who shows himself as Absolute Love, pours himself forth as absolute Good, and in that way definitively utters the absolute Truth. God shows himself as the ab-

---

68. St Augustine, *Confessions*, x, 43: '*faciens tibi nos de servis filios de te (Patre) nascendo, tibi serviendo.*' (Translation my own).
69. Aidan Nichols OP, *Scribe of the Kingdom*, II, London 1994, 26.

solute Beauty, gives himself as the absolute Good, and speaks himself as the absolute Truth.[70] Christianity begins to stand forth as a threefold of theological aesthetic, theological dramatic, and theological logic. For this reason 'Christianity is destroyed if it lets itself be reduced to transcendental presuppositions of a man's self-understanding whether in thought or in life, in knowledge or in action.'[71] It is also destroyed if it lets itself be reduced to being an answer to the search of history or the goal of the elan of the world. Christ in fact is the answer that questions all answers, the omega point that wildly exceeds 'all that we could dare ask or imagine' (Eph 3:20). He lets his glory be seen and the result is that the eyes of our hearts are healed (St Augustine), and enabled both to believe 'into Christ' (Jn 2:11; see 11:40; 19:37; 1 Jn 1:1-3) and to be drawn into communion with the Father of the incarnate Son. (Jn 14: 6-7; 1 Jn 1:2-3)

The Old Testament carried a particularly severe prohibition against the making of idols (Ex 20: 4-5; Lev 19:4; Hos 8:6; Deut 4:35; 6:4). With the advance of revelation it was increasingly clear why it did so: men and women could make God only in their own image and likeness. Only God himself could manifest himself. He had to be his own exegete.[72] In the words of a contemporary philosopher, 'The incarnation of divine order within reality can never be adequately manifested by the imperfect, creaturely struggle for realisation. Only God himself can reveal the meaning of his order within time.'[73] It is God himself who, revealing himself as glory, shows that 'the theological object provides the conditions of possibility for its knowledge.'[74] Here ultimately is the reason why von Balthasar focuses on the revealed cipher of glory, which correlates with beauty. This permits him to propose a genuinely 'theological theology' as a solid

70. See Hans Urs von Balthasar, *Epilog*, Einsiedeln 1988, *passim*.
71. Hans Urs von Balthasar, *Love Alone the way of Revelation*, New York 1968, 43.
72. *Idem*, 'God is his own Exegete', in *Communio*, XIII, 4 (1986), 280-6.
73. David Walsh, *The Third Millennium: Reflections on Faith and Reason*, Washington DC, 1999, 126.
74. John O'Donnell, *Hans Urs von Balthasar*, London 1992, 21.

alternative to a merely anthropological unpacking of divine revelation.[75]

b. Towards a Trinitarian Ontology: Hemmerle

The implications of revelation for metaphysics are striking. And they must be so if divine revelation is to be perceived in its pristine freshness and have cultural significance. Since 'God is love' (1 Jn 4:8, 16), a new metaphysics has to evolve. This metaphysics has to incorporate the revealed principle that Being at its summit is love, indeed trinitarian love. Henri de Lubac makes the point with vigour: 'The mystery of the Trinity has opened to us a totally new perspective: the ground of being is communio.'[76] In the fourth century this was clear to a thinker such as Gregory Nazianzen when he wrote: 'Unity having from all eternity arrived by motion at Duality, found its rest in Trinity. This is what we mean by Father and Son and Holy Ghost.'[77] Here one notices the event of the Trinity as the core of what is specifically Christian. In the following century, St Augustine would have liked to develop his *De trinitate* in strictly interpersonal terms. He suggests the explosive potential of Christian revelation for our understanding of Being at all its echelons when he wrote, 'If you see charity, you see the Trinity.'[78] The God of Jesus Christ is not a One who wants to substitute the Many. Rather, he wishes 'to lead the many to the Trinity. Jesus has opened out for us the One of the Trinity.'[79] Bonaventure in his time designed the whole of his theological enterprise under the rubric of the Trinity.[80] Pascal saw this vividly in the sixteenth century when

75. Klaus Hemmerle, *Thesen zu einer trinitarischen Ontologie*, in *Ausgewählten Schriften*, Band 2, Freiburg-Basel-Wien 1996, 124-161.
76. Henri de Lubac, *La Foi chrétienne*, Paris 1970, 14.
77. Gregory Nazianzen, *The Third Theological Oration*, 2, in *The Nicene and Post-Nicene Fathers*, vol VII, Grand Rapids and Michigan 1974, 301.
78. St Augustine, *De Trinitate*, 'Imo vero vides Trinitatem, si caritatem vides', VIII, 8, 12: PL 42, 958; see also VIII, 10.
79. Giuseppe Zanghí, 'A Reflection on Postmodernity', in *Being One*, 7 (1998), 83.
80. St Bonaventure, *De triplici via*, c2 s3 n8, *Opera Omnia. Tomus VIII*.

he wrote: 'A plurality that cannot be integrated into unity is chaos; unity unrelated to plurality is tyranny.'[81] These great figures, however, are exceptions proving that the revolutionary meaning of revelation has not been drawn out in the received theological and philosophical tradition.

Now here we are face-to-face with both a deficit and a drama. The deficit consists in the absence of an ontology responsive to a revelation whose core insight is that the summit of reality is a Tri-unity. Klaus Hemmerle describes this deficit vividly in his *Thesen zu einer trinitarischen Ontologie*: 'The basic concern of an ontology which would set out from what is specifically Christian can no longer be the question, what remains and what changes? This question may not be omitted, but it is a question that can no longer constitute an indisputable point of departure. For if the enterprise of thought is grounded exclusively on that which remains, one begins from an isolated point of departure and with the desire of defending one's own positions and one's own purposes.'[82] In a word, the basic Christian revelation and experience simply demands 'a new understanding of Being.'[83]

Christian revelation shows that God is Trinity, and that each of the Divine Persons is in the Others and for the Others, as the Fathers expressed so clearly with their idea of *perichoresis*. Christian revelation, furthermore, stresses the axiom that only the person who loses his life for the gospel (Mk 8:35) and for others (Mt 25:30-45) will find it.

It is difficult to exaggerate the revolutionary impact of the

---

Quaracchi 1898, 9f; and the commentary-article by Hanspeter Heinz, 'Dreifaltige Liebe-Gekreuzigte Liebe', in *Wissenschaft und Weisheit*, (1984), 12-22. In this context it is fascinating to read Bonaventure's definition of the Church, *'Ecclesia enim mutuo se diligens est'*, *Hexaemeron*, I, 4.

81. Pascal, *Pensées*, ed, Chevalier, 809: as quoted in Hans Urs von Balthasar, *The Office of Peter and the Structure of the Church*, San Francisco 1986, 21.

82. Klaus Hemmerle, *Thesen zu einer trinitarischen Ontologie*, 140: translation my own.

83. Klaus Kienzler, *'Zu den Anfangen einer "trinitarischen Ontologie"'* in *Der dreieine Gott und die eine Menscheit*, Freiburg-Basel-Wien 1989, 45.

simple affirmation that only love lasts. For if what lasts is
love, then the centre of gravity shifts from the self to the
other, and both movement (not in the Aristotelian sense) and
relationship (*relatio*, no longer understood as a category, as
the most insignificant accident of Being) go to the centre of
the stage. Movement and relationship, however, do not constitute a new principle from which everything could again be
derived by means of an isolated deduction. Only one thing
remains, participation in that movement which love (*Agape*)
itself is. This movement is the very rhythm of Being. It is the
rhythm of that giving which gives itself.[84]

The deficit in ontology, however, is the key to an historical
drama that continues to unfold in the West. That drama may be
detected in the atomisation of Christian society, and in the conviction widespread even among Christians that the revelation of
God as Trinity has nothing to do with personal living or the
building up of society in solidarity. It is enough to think of the
notion of the human person that holds sway in order to see the
truth of Hemmerle's diagnosis and the need for an antidote.
That notion was formulated by Boethius, and has become theologically and socially dominant. The person is an individual, a
'*naturae rationalis individua substantia*', and not also a capacity
crying out for communion and relationship.[85] Yet Augustine
had understood a divine Person as *relatio*, and Aquinas as *relatio
subsistens*. Perhaps it is the dominance of person as individual
over person as relation that is the real reason for the slowness
with which the Council's emphasis on communion is being received in the church.

This chapter set out to revisit the teaching of the Second
Vatican Council on revelation. It did so, however, with a very
definite purpose in view. Having studied the 'two languages'

---

84. Hemmerle, *ibid.*, 141.
85. Boethius, *Liber de persona et duabus naturis*, 3: PL 64, 1343. This definition initiated the progressive abandonment of the relational dimension
of personality, '*così centrale nella nozione trinitaria di persona*', Luis F.
Ladaria, *Antropologia Teologica*, Asti 1998, 15.

operative in the text in order to highlight the new 'style' of life now emerging in the church, it listed five major breakthroughs in the text of the first two chapters of *Dei Verbum*. It then went on to propose some elaboration of each of those areas. In a concluding section it mentioned two omissions in the text, the one theological and the other philosophical in character. Christian revelation consists above all in the glory-beauty of trinitarian, crucified and glorified Love shown and offered to humankind as our very *Lebensraum* already here and now (1 Jn 3:2). Such a disclosure of 'the love of Christ which is beyond all knowledge' (Eph 3:19) must transform our understanding of reality and inspire the elaboration of a trinitarian ontology as the 'handmaid of Catholic theology'. That is why we shall have to return to this topic in our fourth chapter where we shall suggest a first sketch of some of the components of such an ontology.

Perhaps the last word should be had by that unknown genius of the early second century when writing to his friend, Diognetus: his elegant words catch the melody that crosses the two millennia of theological reflection on divine revelation.

> It is not an earthly discovery that has been entrusted to the Christians. The thing they guard so jealously is no product of mortal thinking, and what has been committed to them is no stewardship of human mysteries. The Almighty himself, the Creator of the Universe, the God whom no eye can discern, has sent down his very own Truth from heaven, his own holy and incomprehensible Word, to plant it among men and ground it in their hearts.[86]

---

86. *The Epistle to Diognetus*, 7, in Maxwell Staniforth (ed), *Early Christian Writers*, London 1968, 178.

CHAPTER TWO

The Law of the Trinity:
the Mutual Gift of Ourselves

Genuine Christian life is an imitation of the Trinity. Just as there is one God in three Persons, so, in Christ, we are all 'members one of another'; there is, and we are called to become, *a single Man in a multitude of persons*.[1]

Something great and momentous is taking place: the programme intended by the Second Vatican Council for the church is beginning to take shape. Could it have taken all of forty years for this 'pastoral Council' to begin to impact the church's life? The answer is to be seen in the history of the church or rather of the ecumenical Councils: time was of the essence in the reception of the various Councils. Theologians and historians speak of a sequence of phases in the reception of the Second Vatican Council.[2] The first phase was one of exuberance. This disposition emerged during the sessions of the Council and dominated the first decade after the Council. The Council was a new beginning. Such was the enthusiasm that the theological debate began to leave the conciliar texts behind.

This phase, however, was soon to be followed by a phase of disappointment. Not all the expectations were fulfilled at once. For example, the notion of the church as *communio* did not become instantly a reality. What does communion actually mean? In the parishes? In the dioceses? What is its relevance in the church's social teaching and action? The radical change affecting

---

1. Olivier Clément, *On Human Being. A Spiritual Anthropology*, New York and London 2000, 44.
2. See Hermann J. Pottmeyer and Walter Kasper, 'The continuing Challenge of the Second Vatican Council' in *Theology & Church*, New York 1989, 166f.

society in general set up its own set of expectations as well. The church had opened her doors to the modern world, but it seemed to many that there was a diluting of what she should then be offering to the men and women entering through those doors. The result was a factious conflict between so-called 'conservatives' and 'progressives', a scenario that vividly recalled the struggle in the church of Corinth in the early decades of the church or the doctrinal confusion that St Basil the Great observed after the first of the ecumenical councils.[3]

The Special Synod which took place in 1985, twenty years after the Council, seemed to initiate a third phase. It succeeded in doing this because it drew attention again to the texts and not only to the slogan, 'the spirit of the Council'. It even went as far as identifying *communio* as the organising principle of the whole Council, the key hermeneutic for the reading of her constitutions and decrees.[4] This had the effect of gradually turning attention to the great principles of the Council, as well as to their reception. This new focus had the good effect of focusing both the disappointed and the disillusioned on the implementation of the Council. Subsequent developments tended in the main to advance this process.

It is significant that in his Apostolic Letter announcing the Great Jubilee, *Tertio Millennio Adveniente*, Pope John Paul proposed a serious examination of conscience to the whole church as the immediate preparation for the Jubilee. He asked Catholics to examine how they had responded to the central and clear teaching of the Council. For example, he asked about our response to *Sacrosanctum Concilium* and the liturgical renewal which it sketched. He asked about the extent to which Catholics

---

3. See Joseph Ratzinger, *Principles of Catholic Theology*, San Francisco 1987, Epilogue 367-393 for a fascinating account of the parallel between the reception of the early fourth-century Councils and that of Vatican II; see *idem, Christmas Discourse to Curia* where he deals with the two conflicting hermeneutics that have slowed the reception of Vatican II: *L'Osservatore Romano*, 23 December 2005.

4. *Extraordinary Synod Final Report 1985*, II.c.1 in *L'Osservatore Romano*, December 10, 1985.

had welcomed the fresh emphasis on knowing and living by the revealed Word of God. These are serious questions, for the good reason that they articulate what the Holy Spirit is saying to the church and the world *in our times*. However, they also require the obedient faith of the church.

At the end of the Jubilee the Pope published *Novo Millennio Ineunte*. This is both a very practical letter and a very visionary one. It not only reiterates the identification of *communio* in the Extraordinary Synod of 1985 as the guiding principle of the whole Council but also proposes a 'spirituality of communion' as the necessary way to bring this *communio* into being. 'To make the church *the home and the school of communion*: that is the great challenge facing us in the millennium which is now beginning, if we wish to be faithful to God's plan and respond to the world's deepest yearnings.' (43) He goes on to explain that this spirituality of communion precedes the 'making of practical plans'. It must guide all levels of formation and all the institutes of formation. It is the way to build up families, parishes and communities. 'A spirituality of communion indicates above all the heart's contemplation of the Trinity dwelling in us, and whose light we must also be able to see shining on the faces of the brothers and sisters around us.' (43)

Such a spirituality flows like a spring of refreshing water from the gospel and is proposed as the spirituality for the whole church since it corresponds to the truth of the church's origin, essence and mission. 'Let us have no illusions: unless we follow this spiritual path, external structures of communion will serve very little purpose. They would become mechanisms without a soul, "masks" of communion rather than its means of expression and growth.' (43) The principle is clear: if Catholics do live as men and women of communion, the projects they undertake and the ministries they perform will be correspondingly enriched.

Rugged Individualism
Now the spirituality that preceded the Council was ruggedly individual. Christ had died to save all, indeed. This meant that 'in

Christ there was neither Jew nor Greek, neither free person nor slave, neither male nor female, for all are one.' (Gal 3:28) For the first Christians, water was thicker than blood! The Fathers saw the mystery of Christ from first to last as a mystery of unity, a fact underlined in their theology of sin as a separation from God and from one another. In overcoming that division, Christ causes a 're-unification of humankind.' 'For when God became man, he drew one man to himself and into unity with God, and in so doing he has attracted the humanity of all men and women ... The humanity of Jesus Christ is at one and the same time the divine fishing-rod (*Angelrute*), which has encountered the one humanity of all men and women, so that the humanity (*Menschsein*) of all men and women is led into the unity of the Body of Christ, the God-Man, and is led out of the death-dealing of that separation which is called sin.'[5]

The Council picked up the same teaching. It taught that 'it has pleased God to save us not as individuals, but as a People.' (*LG* 9) Still, the way to the Father's house for most Christians in recent centuries was not in company but on one's own. It was not the way of a great contemporary Christian who would write: 'God comes down into me by way of bread (the Eucharist): I go up to him by way of my brother ... Your love made me discover my brothers; they were the *viaticum* for always climbing from earth to heaven.' The 'mystery of love' is 'God, my neighbour, I.'[6]

The Communion of Saints, to take a further example, was for the next world. But entry into the communion was a very personal pilgrimage. The Council in its *Constitution on the Church*, however, included a whole chapter on the eschatological nature of the church and her union with the church in heaven. Christianity is an eschatology as much as, and perhaps even more than, it is an epiclesis of the Holy Spirit re-presenting the wonders of God in salvation history. In the Christian life there is

---

5. Joseph Ratzinger, *Die Einheit der Nationen. Eine Vision der Kirchenväter*, Salzburg 1971, 31, 32, 33.
6. Igino Giordani, *The Diary of Fire*, London 1982, entries for 14 April 1960; 8 December 1973.

an 'already now' that participates in the 'still not yet'. (1 Jn 3:2)
But this was a vision so unintelligible that it was not even heard
as a message and an imperative for daily living. The spiritual
journey was an individual one. True, the community could help,
indeed, had to help. But in the final analysis the way was utterly
an individual one. Catholicism, the most social of all religions,
had in fact become an individual 'way'.

The eminent German Jesuit, Fr Karl Rahner, wrote in 1983 on
the spirituality of the church of the future. His central contention
is worth quoting: 'Those of us who are older ... have been spirit-
ually formed in an individualist way ... If there ever was an experience of the Spirit that took place among people as a group
and is normally understood as such ... it is the experience of the
first Pentecost in the church, an event – we must presume – that
certainly did not consist in the casual meeting of a collection of
mystics who lived individually, but in the experience of the
Spirit had by the community ... I think that in a future spirituality
the element of a fraternal spiritual communion, of a spirituality
lived together, would play a more decisive role, and that slowly
but surely we must go in this direction.'[7]

The question arises at once, how did this 'individualist way'
come about? A complete answer is outside the scope of this
book. However, part of the answer lies in the fact that the sense
of Christianity as communion is directly dependent on the realisation that God is a communion because he is a Trinity. The sense
of the Trinity had diminished in the church. The claim of Karl
Rahner is well known. According to him, 'despite their orthodox
confession of the Trinity, Christians are, in their practical life, almost mere "monotheists". We must be willing to admit that,
should the doctrine of the Trinity have to be dropped as false,
the major part of religious literature could well remain virtually
unchanged.'[8]

---

7. Karl Rahner, 'Elementi di spiritualità nella Chiesa del futuro' in Problemi e
prospettive di spiritualità, edited by T. Goffi and B. Secondin, Brescia
1983, 440-441.
8. Karl Rahner, The Trinity, trs Joseph Donceel, London 1970, 10-11.

No sincere Christian, of course, would have wanted to deny the fact of the Trinity or delete it from his faith horizon. But it had no practical relevance to the life that Christians should live together in order to witness the Risen Christ to the world. (Jn 13:35; 17:21) The philosopher, Immanuel Kant, was right after all in his claim that the doctrine of the Trinity has no connection with everyday life.[9] True, no Christian would have denied the 'economic principle' that we go *to* the Father *through* his beloved Son and *in* their Holy Spirit. But this was the vertical way, and did not suggest any kind of reciprocity among those on the same 'heroic adventure of the soul'. True again, in the public arena of the liturgy we would be careful to observe a prepositional propriety: 'Through him, with him and in him is to you, God the Father, in the unity of the Holy Spirit all honour and glory.' But that we are a 'people made one from the unity of the Father, the Son, and the Holy Spirit' was only rarely adverted to in the preconciliar period.

The theology or understanding of the Trinity, besides, was confined to the 'psychological analogy'. This inevitably led to a 'being locked into oneself' (*Ichgeschlossenheit*), a state of affairs where the understanding of the highest mystery of the faith not only harmonised with an individualistic way but actually reinforced it. God the Holy Trinity lived in individual Christians, but it did not generally occur to anyone that he lived in others too in order to form 'a people made one from the unity of the Father, the Son and the Holy Spirit.'[10] In this perspective, the Holy Trinity formed the church, as the very We-structure of the Creed witnesses.[11]

More than a 'Pastoral Council'
The Council, however, was more than a 'pastoral' council, even allowing for latitude in the connotation of the word 'pastoral'. It

---

9. Immanuel Kant, *Il conflitto delle facoltà*, Italian translation, Genoa 1953, 47.
10. St Cyprian, *De oratione dominica*, 23: PL 4, 553.
11. See Joseph Ratzinger, *Principles*, 15-55.

was also a great theological event. It was such because the
Council very deliberately put theological questions high on the
scale of its priorities. It wanted to speak to the hearts of modern
men and women from out of the depths of 'the faith given once
for all to the saints'. (Jude 3) It wisely sought the right mode for
such an address and the appropriate dress, as John XXIII memorably stressed in his opening *allocutio*.[12] This concern, however,
did not distract the Council from an adequate treatment of the
central components of faith. Many authors stress this perhaps
forgotten dimension. Their central contention is that the Council
did address central areas of faith such as Christ, revelation,
Trinity, church and eucharist. To these it imparted new impulse.
In doing so the Council showed itself to be in fine tune with the
singularly brilliant theologians, liturgists, patrologists and historians who had prepared the Council by their research even as
they resourced the Council while it was in progress.

To take just one example, there was the extraordinary work
of Henri de Lubac, *Catholicism. On the Social Aspects of Dogma*.
First published in 1938, it distilled the essence of the church's
tradition, patristic, medieval and modern, and combined it with
the wisdom of the ages. De Lubac had succeeded in writing a
work that showed up the essentially social character of Catholic
dogma, as well as the preoccupation of Catholicism with the
unity of humankind.[13] His insight, which was typical of the
work done by towering theologians of the time, flowed into the
texts of the Council.

The Separation of Spirituality and Theology
John Henry Newman has famously remarked on the aftermath
of the ecumenical councils of the church. Two facts stand out for
the church historian. First, there is the fact of the turmoil and
sometimes the rather disedifying posturing of certain protagon-
ists in the course of the Council itself. Second, there is the turbul-

12. Pope John XXIII, *Opening Speech to the Council*, 1962 in Abbott, *The
Documents of Vatican II*, London 1966, 710-719.
13. Henri de Lubac, *Catholicism. The Social Aspects of Dogma*, London
1950. See the comments of Pope Benedict in the encyclical *Spe Salvi*, 13.

ence during the decades following the council when doctrine seems to slip, liturgy seems to pander to the private whims of congregations and individuals, and morality and church order are disturbed as if in a hurricane. In due course, however, true order returns and what was sown in tears bears the harvest the Lord had intended in first calling the Council.[14]

There is a further factor that has entered the equation, however: during the past millennium, at least since the decline of the great scholastic movement culminating in the thirteenth century, there has been a debilitating separation of spirituality and theology. This means that since roughly the end of the fifteenth century the theologians are on one road while the great spirituals are on another. The two roads have diverged drastically. The passing of time has exacerbated the separation. Hans Urs von Balthasar makes the point vividly: 'a strange anatomical dissection: on the one hand, the bones without the flesh, "traditional theology"; on the other, the flesh without bones, that very pious literature that serves up a compound of asceticism, mysticism, spirituality and rhetoric, a porridge that, in the end, becomes indigestible through lack of substance.'[15] Theology suffers as a result of its distance from spirituality and religious experience. Spirituality for its part loses its vitality as a result of its subtle disconnection from the solid meat of the content of faith (*fides quae*). The two disciplines impoverish each other mutually.

This has damaged the cause of preaching the gospel effectively. The phenomenon of our times whereby many people in the West go in search of experts in other faiths for guidance towards God and the interior world brings home the fact that the dogmas of the church have not been nourishing faith, while the spirituality(ies) have not been looking to the substance of divine revelation for much of their discourse. True theology is 'an act of

---

14. See Ian Ker, 'Newman, the Councils, and Vatican II', *Communio*, XXVIII, 4 (2001), 708-728.
15. Hans Urs von Balthasar, 'Theology and Sanctity' in *Word and Redemption, Essays in Theology 2*, New York 1965, 49-86, here 65.

adoration and prayer,' a praying theology, while spirituality for its part is 'the subjective aspect of dogma.'[16]

It was the conviction of Cardinal Newman that 'theology is the fundamental and regulating principle of the whole church system.'[17] As the expression of the prophetical office of the church, it oversees the exercise of the sanctifying and regal offices. However, a theology that is not rooted in the Word of God, a theology that does not nourish, inspire and guide the faith-life of believers, can be but a poor 'regulating' principle. When Newman thought of theology he tended to gravitate towards theology as crafted by the Fathers. That theology had a life to it. St Augustine, for example, could typically state its arête with the two dialectical principles, *'Credo ut intelligam'* ('I believe in order to understand') and *'Intelligo ut credam'* ('I understand in order to believe').[18] The rather arid theology of some schools of neo-scholasticism in the twentieth century had the effect of distancing many seekers of God from the world of theology: if you want to encounter the God of Jesus Christ, do not study theology! The anti-intellectualism of some Catholics may perhaps be attributed to this experience.

The Legacy that is to be Lived

God reveals and communicates himself to us so that we 'might have life and have it in abundance.'(Jn 10:10) The goal and the scope of part two of this essay is to bring out the wonder of that revelation in 'the unfathomable riches of Christ.' (Eph 3:8) Hearing it is designed to lead to faith, believing it to hope, and hoping it to love.[19] He does not reveal himself so that we should merely *know* more but rather that we should *do* better in living the one life we have. Christianity, in other words, is eminently a

---

16. *Ibid.*, 87-88.
17. John Henry Newman, *Preface to the Third Edition of the Via Media*, London 1901, xlvii.
18. St Augustine, *Sermo* 43, 9: PL 38, 258. Pope John Paul II employs these correlative principles when discussing the rapport of faith and reason in his encyclical *Fides et Ratio*, chapters two and three.
19. See *Dei Verbum* 1.

practical religion: it sets before us revealed facts and truths and ordinances and leaves the announcement of these to make their impact upon such people as are actually prepared for that announcement. In Christ is life. Whoever receives that life does not die. This 'life is the light of humankind'. (Jn 1:4) It is a life that the Son has brought from the bosom of the Trinity. (Jn 1:18) It is identical with the Son made flesh who is that life made flesh. (Jn 14:6; 6:57) To receive this life, however, we have to relegate what we often believe to be life but which is in fact mere counterfeit.

Conversion, in a word, is the pre-requisite on the human side to enter into the life offered in Christ, the life that lasts forever. (Jn 6:51f) The life that we lead may be only a form of death. (Lk 9:59-60) Jesus began the preaching of the gospel with the declaration that the kingdom of God is present so that the only logical attitude is to displace all the idols occupying the centre of one's being, the heart, and to replace them with that kingdom as both gift and mission. This dynamic of displacement-replacement is the very core of the gospel message. It is what the gospels call 'repentance.' (Mk 1:14-15)[20] God comes from the periphery to the centre. He comes to the only place that he may properly occupy. Otherwise, his kingdom does not come, his name is not hallowed in our hearts, and his will is not done on earth as it is in heaven. (Mt 6:9-10)

The foundation of authentic religion, then, is conversion. Such conversion has a sequence of levels that are dynamically interconnected, as Bernard Lonergan demonstrates. There is religious conversion which 'is being grasped by ultimate concern. It is other-worldly falling in love. It is total and permanent self-surrender without conditions, qualifications, reservations ... For Christians it is God's love flooding our hearts through the Holy Spirit given to us. It is the gift of grace.'[21] Religious conversion is a modality of self-transcendence ... to a total being-in-love as the efficacious ground of all self-transcendence, whether in the pur-

---

20. See Klaus Hemmerle, *Glauben – wie geht das?*, Freiburg-im-Breisgau, 1978, 21-34.
21. Bernard Lonergan, *Method in Theology*, London 1972, 240-1.

suit of truth, or in the realisation of human values, or in the orientation man adopts to the universe, its ground, and its goal.'[22] The outcome of such conversion is that the Holy Spirit and the human spirit encounter profoundly. Then there occurs that convergence to which St Paul refers with the words, 'The Spirit himself and our spirit bear united witness that we are children of God.' (Rom 8:17)

Religious conversion brings in its wake moral conversion, as St Augustine famously demonstrated in the *Confessions*.[23] For the operative grace changing the heart of stone to be a heart of flesh (Jer 31:33) now 'changes the criterion of one's decisions and choices from satisfactions to values.'[24] Since love has eyes, as Aquinas so perceptively stressed, the eyes of the love of the Holy Spirit flooding our hearts 'reveals values in their splendour, while the strength of this love brings about their realisation.'[25] In the words of Cardinal Newman, 'Truth there is, and attainable it is, but its rays stream in upon us through the medium of our moral as well as our intellectual being.'[26] At this level of conversion one becomes acutely aware 'that it is up to each of us to decide for himself what he is to make of himself'. Of course, moral conversion 'falls far short of moral perfection. Deciding is one thing, doing is another.'[27]

If religious conversion is conversion to the source of all love and goodness and value, and moral conversion is to values, intellectual conversion is to the value of truth. The first dimension of intellectual conversion is the conviction that the mind is made for truth, that truth is an essential colour of reality, and that the mind can reach truth albeit with effort and then in varying measures. Intellectual conversion recognises the 'thrust ... of intelli-

---

22. *Ibid.*, 241.
23. See my *Newman and his Theological Method. A Guide for the Theologian Today*, Leiden 1977, chapter IV, 'Theology and its Methodical Foundations,' 84-111.
24. Bernard Lonergan, *ibid.*, 240.
25. *Ibid.*, 243.
26. John Henry Newman, *A Grammar of Assent*, London 1870, 304.
27. Bernard Lonergan, *ibid.*, 240.

gence to the intelligible, of reasonableness to the true and the real.'[28] Since we live in an era that is dominated by 'weak reason', the importance of intellectual conversion takes on even further importance. In the practical or existential order, intellectual conversion follows moral conversion, for a person who dislikes values and the good is not going to be interested in the truth, as Plato has famously demonstrated.[29]

'What the Spirit is saying to the Church'

During the Council, the church identified the law of her being and existence. In the *Constitution on the Church*, one reads that 'the law [of the People of God] is the new commandment to love as Christ loved us. (Jn 13:34)' (9) This occurs in a passage of rare beauty describing the church as the People of God. The reference to the text of the New Commandment is not without significance, as we shall shortly discover. In the *Pastoral Constitution on the Church in the Modern World* the New Commandment is again put forward in the context of human activity viewed in the light of the paschal mystery. The relevant portion of the paragraph deserves quoting: '[God's Word] himself revealed that "God is love" (1 Jn 4:8). At the same time he taught us that the new command of love was the basic law of human perfection and hence of the world's transformation.' (38) The New Commandment which lies at the core of New Testament revelation is identified as indispensable to the church, human perfection and the genuine renewal of the world.

The same Council also identified *koinonia* as vitally important for the life of the church. Called by many 'the guiding idea'[30] of the Council, the word and the idea feature prominently in the texts of the Council. A richness of content accompanies the word. Thus communion involves a communion with God. In fact, it consists in a participation in God through word and

---

28. *Ibid.*, 115-6.
29. See Plato, *The Gorgias:* for a commentary see Eric Voegelin, *Order and History, III, Plato and Aristotle*, Baton Rouge 1957, 24-45.
30. For example, Walter Kasper, *Theology & Church*, 149.

sacrament. '… the Greek word *koinonia* (Latin *communio*) does not originally mean "community" at all. It means participation, and more particularly, in the good things of salvation conferred by God: participation in the Holy Spirit, in new life, in love, in the gospel, but above all participation in the eucharist.'[31]

The Law of Life for the Church: the New Commandment

C. S. Lewis has famously described the varieties of love in *The Four Loves*.[32] The highest form of love is that of *agape* which subsumes and sublimates the previous levels. This is the uniquely Christian form and has been the object of many excellent studies in recent decades.[33] The linguistic clue to its originality is the fact that *agape* is rarely used in classical Greek (only under the form of *agapan*) but is frequently used in the translation of the Old Testament into the koine Greek of Alexandria. This prepares the way for a specifically biblical and Christian meaning of the word. The zenith of this development may be read in the Book of Glory of St John's gospel (chapters 13-17). There one encounters the summit of divine revelation which is articulated in terms of *agape*. It is to this 'book' that we should now turn in order to discover its inspiration and guidance for everyday living.

St John's mode of thought is unique. It is a spiralling thinking and writing, 'like a winding staircase always revolving around the same centre, always recurring to the same topics, but at a higher level.'[34] We will follow that staircase in its ascent to the summit of the love-life of Christians. With the supper just beginning and Jesus having washed the feet of the disciples, Jesus announces to them something utterly original. He speaks in fact of a commandment which is 'his' and is 'new'.

---

31. *Ibid.*, 154.
32. C. S. Lewis, *The Four Loves*, London 1960.
33. See C. Spicq, *Agape dans le nouveau testament, I,II*, Paris 1965; P. Foresi, *L'agape in San Paolo e la carità in San Tommaso d'Aquino*, Roma 1965.
34. Ignace de la Potterie, *Adnotationes in Exegesim Primae Epistulae S. Joannis*, Pontificium Institutum Biblicum, Romae 1967, 8; see also Michael Mullins, *The Gospel of John*, Dublin 2003.

I give you a new commandment,
that you love one another.
Just as I have loved you, you also love one another. (13:34)

In the Old Covenant there was the promise of the New Covenant. This promise stood out most prominently in the prophets, particularly in Jeremiah and Ezechiel. The classical instance is in Jeremiah 31:31-33. The new law for the New Covenant was no longer going to be graven on tablets of stone as with the Mosaic Covenant (Ex 2:16). It was going to be written on the heart. The 'new' commandment is one of mutual love: mutuality is of its very essence. Already in the First Testament, in fact in the Law, there were the prescriptions to love God with all one's heart (Deut 6:5) and to love the neighbour as oneself. (Lev 19:18) With Jesus, however, an absolutely original dimension enters, that of commandment as a real sharing in the law of mutual love governing the being and living of the Father and Jesus.

Mutuality admits of degree, and so Jesus specifies the measure of this mutual love. It is a measure which is given by his very example: 'as I have loved you.' A measure, then, that is without measure. The word, 'as' (*kathos*), is one of those New Testament words that brings out the attractiveness of the things of God. Here it has the meaning of likeness, prolongation of, and assimilation to, the love of Jesus.[35] In our very next chapter we shall have occasion to follow out in detail the meaning and the import of that 'as', illustrating its scope through a series of plunges into key moments of Christian history. Here the 'as' refers rearwards to the opening phrase of the Book of Glory, 'Now before the festival of the Passover, Jesus knew that his hour had come to depart from this world and go to the Father. Having loved his own who were in this world, he loved them *to the end.*' (13:1)

Not only is there reference to the Father, but also to the context of all that is about to happen in his own passover to the

---

35. C. Spicq, *ibid.*, 173f.

Father, a passover that is going to involve his death on the wood of the cross. Christian love is a love without limits, without measure, without conditions. Existentially costing not less than everything, it will locate the divine, the *agape of the Father and the Son*, in the world of men and women. When that reality ensouls the relationships of believers, everyone will know that Christ has authentic disciples in the world. (13:35) 'Jesus brought into history a completely new depth to interpersonal relations, both as an ideal to be aimed at and as a reality for whoever wishes to respond to his invitation to make absolutely unconditional love the norm of their lives.'[36]

We can climb a step or two up the spiralling staircase constructed by the evangelist. In chapter fifteen, verses 9-15, Jesus employs the analogue of the love existing between the Father and himself as the key to his love for them: 'As the Father has loved me, so I have loved you.' (9) The *agape* bonding the Father and the Son is explicitly extended to the disciples. Then the allegory of the Vine and the Branches is effectively employed to underscore the import and the consequence of such unity in terms of mutual indwelling or 'co-personal presence'. 'Just as the branch cannot bear fruit by itself unless it abides in the vine, neither can you unless you abide in me. I am the vine, you are the branches. Those who abide in me and I in them bear much fruit ...' (4b-5)

The new commandment may now return at this higher level. It is the love obtaining eternally between the Father and the Son, just as we have seen, but John enables us to deepen our grasp of the *as*: 'No one has greater love than this, to lay down one's life for one's friends.' (13) To live by the new commandment of Jesus requires Christians not only to be committed to each other, but under no circumstances to break their link with each other. In other words, they must be willing to lay down their lives for each other as the Master has done for each of them.

Now it is here that we are sometimes quite appalled at the

---

36. Brendan M. Purcell, *The Drama of Humanity*, Frankfurt am Main 1996, 168.

lack of love that we show. When Jesus announces his readiness to love 'to the end', we are happy to accept. It is fine if he will do it! We accept. But what is the quality of our commitment to others? It is in reflecting on this that we discover our own frigidity, and realise that, egoists that we are, we have no true love.[37] That realisation causes a searing pain, but it may be the beginning of conversion, at least to desire to live the new commandment. To desire is to be already within the reality brought by Jesus from the Father. There is, besides, a very practical implication of this revelation. 'Since reciprocal love between persons is the highest form of love for Jesus, a man's laying down his life out of love for others who fully appreciate and love him is a greater fulfilment of love than an act of love which either passes unappreciated by others or must await their response.'[38] This is the revelation of a divine depth in interpersonal relations which Jesus has brought into history. It was not in existence heretofore, and none greater can ever be given. In our next stop on the staircase, which is in fact the top, we shall see the ultimate identity of this revelation.

In chapter seventeen, Jesus turns to the Father instead of speaking directly to the disciples. We are aware of an invitation to eavesdrop on a conversation between the Son and the Father. The theme of that conversation is unity, the fruit of the new commandment when it is lived in the way that Jesus has explained in his teaching and will illustrate in his cross as his love to the end in 'the hour.' (2:4; 13:1; 17:1) The form and dynamics of that unity are drawn out twice over in verses 21 to 24. It is possible to detect a fivefold parallel between 21a–22a and 22b–24ab. The two sets of text should be set out to facilitate easy reading, and easy reading will help in the shredding of their riches:

---

37. Hans Urs von Balthasar, *Love Alone the Way of Revelation*, London 1968, 51.
38. Brendan M. Purcell, *ibid.*, 168.

21a 'That all may be one.

   21b As you, Father, are in me and I am in you,

      21c may they also be in us,

         21d so that the world may believe you have sent me.

            22a The glory that you have given me I have given them.'

22b 'That they may be one

   22c as we are one.

      23ab I in them and you in me,

      that they may become perfectly one,

         23cd so that the world may know that you have sent me and have loved them even as you have loved me.

            24ab Father, I want those you have given me to be with me where I am, so that they may always see the glory you have given me.'

Jesus turns to the Father and prays for the unity of his disciples (21a and 22b). John interestingly uses the neuter substantive, *hen*, 'one thing', to emphasise the concrete character of the unity he desires. 'The unity that is to be the fruit of the mutual love demanded of the disciples is so great a thing, so close to the heart of Jesus and the Father, and so central to the mission Jesus received from his Father, that Jesus does not entrust it directly to the disciples, but to his Father. And he entrusts it in prayer.'[39] The model of the unity is indicated in the second component (21b and 22c) as the unity between the Son and the Father. However, the unity of the believers is not going to be only a certain likeness to that of the divine Persons, but also a real participation in this very unity (21c and 23ab). They will become a 'we' that participates in the eternal 'We' of the Father and the Son.[40]

The fruit of this life of unity will be just as extraordinary as its own life: it will make the disciples effective witnesses to all men

39. Thomas Norris, 'Why the Marriage of Christians is one of the Seven Sacraments,' in *The Irish Theological Quarterly*, 1 (1985), 42.
40. See Hans Urs von Balthasar, *Herrlichkeit*, III/2, ii, Einsiedeln 1969, 363-404.

and women (21d and 23c). This witness is simply the effect of the unity of the disciples participating in the unity of the blessed Trinity. Living in unity, as 'reinforced' by the prayer of Jesus, they will shout out the truth that the Father exists and that he has sent his beloved Son into the world for the life of the world (3:16; 6:51; 21d; 22cd). The Second Vatican Council very understandably saw in this prayer of Jesus an 'opening up of vistas closed to human reason. For Jesus implied a certain likeness between the union of the divine Persons, and in the union of God's sons in truth and charity. This likeness reveals that man, who is the only creature on earth which God willed for itself, cannot fully find himself except through a sincere gift of himself.'[41]

In the fifth component Jesus announces that he has given the glory he has eternally from the Father to the disciples. Glory as the radiance of Trinitarian, crucified and glorified love, the revealed counterpart of beauty, will irradiate the company of the disciples. This irradiation has already begun (22a), indeed, but its final manifestation may only be received in the future (24b). As the beauty of Jesus' homeland, the Trinity, it will enrapture as soon as it is perceived. Naturally, not all eyes will see nor all hears hear. As we have stressed in this chapter, divine revelation expressed the divine freedom but has to encounter and engage with human created freedom. In this encounter, there is the drama of human existence. The *agape* and the glory that loved us first address our very existence. Still, it is up to us to hear and to welcome that address. Such welcome is what constitutes conversion, and conversion is the foundation of all religion, as we have seen.

Be What you Are!

We have been looking at the summit of divine revelation in what exegetes often call 'The Book of Glory'. Very significantly the context is that of the supper where Jesus institutes the eucharist. John, however, as the last of the gospel writers and speaking to the community of believers in Ephesus, simply assumes the fact of

---

41. *The Church in the Modern World*, 24.

that institution but *sets out to show its existential implications for the life of the Christian community.* This must be the meaning of the 'liturgy' of word and deed in the washing of the feet at the very outset of the discourse: 'If I then, the Lord and Master, have washed your feet, you should wash each other's feet.' (13:14)

Presupposed in all of this is the fact of the eucharist. One cannot live as a child of God (1 Jn 3:10) without the grace of God, and one cannot live eucharistically without first being eucharistised. This explains why John has already presented the eucharist in chapter six as one of those six 'signs' constituting 'The Book of Signs' of his gospel. Using the pattern of miracle, resulting debate and concluding teaching, Jesus multiplies the loaves and fishes to feed the multitude, only to precipitate a populist desire that would make him king by acclamation. This enables him to introduce the discourse on the Bread of Life, which climbs up relentlessly to the shocking teaching on 'the living bread which has come down from heaven'. This living bread is nothing less than 'his flesh given for the life of the world.' (51) In verse fifty-seven Jesus says:

Just as the living Father sent me,
and I live because of the Father,
so whoever eats me
will live because of me.

The eucharistic food and drink take the life existing between the Father and the Son and re-locate it, as it were, on earth and as the most wondrous life uniting those who will eat and drink the gift of God. The communion between the Father and the Son who is nearest the Father's heart (1:18) builds the communion of believers with the Father and with one another. The eucharist is instituted to communicate the life among the Persons of the Trinity to men and women, and in that way men and women enter into this amazing space opened to them by God the Holy Trinity. As Henri de Lubac has shown, 'the eucharist makes the church' even as 'the church makes the eucharist.'[42] However, it

---

42. Cf de Lubac, *Corpus Mysticum. L'Eucharistie et l'Église au Moyen Age,* 2nd Edition, Paris 1949.

is important to think of this church as the communion of *the Blessed Three brought down to earth for the life of the humankind.*

We are now in a position to appreciate the teaching of Jesus on mutual love in the Book of Glory. The disciples have become this new communion through the eucharist, this new 'One Thing' resulting from the 'all'. (17:21) However, there is a vital step to be made: they must live by their new identity. Or to use the recurring phrase of the Fathers, they must *be* what they *are*. Only the eucharist divinises, or rather Christens, and only this enables them to begin to live the new life. The contours of that new life are the contours of what we have called 'the law of the Trinity'. The eucharistic body and blood make them the Body of Christ with the capacity to live a new life, but Jesus has both to show this life in action in the washing of the feet and teach the art of translating it into practical expression in his great discourse. In the delightful words of St Augustine, 'The Lord makes sure of love so as firmly to establish unity.'[43]

What I mean is this. To live the new commandment, which is the law of the Trinity, one has first to be Christ. This is what the eucharist does, as the whole tradition teaches. 'The proper effect of the eucharist is the transformation of man into God,'[44] or his divinisation. St Thomas is here thinking of Leo the Great who writes, 'Our participation in the body and blood of Christ causes us to be transformed into that which we believe and with all fullness we carry, in our spirit and in our flesh, he in whom we are dead, buried and risen.'[45] When the Second Vatican Council wrote its treatise on the church, it underlined the theology of Trinitarian communion[46] and explained this communion as a fruit of the eucharist, since 'the sharing in the body and blood of Christ has no other effect than to accomplish our transformation into that which we receive.' (12) Each one, then, is made into Christ, and all are made into the same Christ. The result is that the many are eucharistised into the one Body, that of the cruci-

43. St Augustine, *Sermo* 56,13; see also *Sermo* 295: PL 38: 1348-1352.
44. St Thomas Aquinas, *In Sent. IV*, dist. 12, q.2, a.1.
45. Leo the Great, *Sermo* 63, 7: PL 54, 357c.
46. Second Vatican Council, *Lumen Gentium*, 26

fied and glorified Christ. How do they live? What is the law of
all laws for those who are the living members of so glorious a
body? A theologian-poet puts the answer splendidly:

I say more: the just man justices;
Keeps grace: that keeps all his goings graces;
Acts in God's eye what in God's eye he is –
Christ.[47]

Now since Christ's whole existence is under the command
received from the Father to give himself (10:18), Christians are
themselves only by loving. Their supreme calling consists in the
imperative to love one another as he has loved them. 'Before all
things, have a constant mutual love.' (1 Pt 4:8) When this is done,
everything is done. If this is not done, then nothing can be done.

St Augustine was quite carried away by this truth. 'If then
you wish to understand the body of Christ, hear what the
Apostle says to believers: "Now you are the body of Christ and
members." (1 Cor 12:27) If therefore you are the body of Christ
and members, your divine mystery is set on the table of the
Lord; you receive your mystery. To that which you are, you answer Amen ... For thou hearest, "The Body of Christ", that thy
Amen may be true. Why then in bread? ... Let us again and
again hear what the Apostle himself says, when speaking of this
Sacrament, "We, being many, are one bread, one body."(1 Cor
10:17) Understand and rejoice: unity, truth, piety, charity.'[48]

From this happy truth flows the imperative of mutual love,
together with the capacity to live by the new commandment.
The law of love among the divine Persons has been brought to
us by the Second Person who has both 'christened' us with the
sacrament and taught us by the gospel of his words and deeds
how to live it. The divine Son knows how difficult the effort to

---

47. Gerard Manley Hopkins, *Poems and Prose*, London 1953, 51: see
Hans Urs von Balthasar's exposition of Hopkins' theology as one of the
outstanding 'lay styles' of theological thought of the second millennium, *The Glory of the Lord, vol III*, Edinburgh 1986, 353-399.
48. St Augustine, *Sermo* 272 as translated in Erich Przywara, *An
Augustine Synthesis*, London 1945, 235.

do so will be unless we are first eucharistised. This enables us to see the great discourse of the supper in John as basically pre-occupied with the law for living eucharistically. It is the eucharist that makes us Christians, *and this enables us to live the law of the Trinity on earth*. We are able to act in the Father's eye what in the Father's eye we are, namely, the one Christ spread out in space and in time. (Gal 3:28)

CHAPTER THREE

Jesus Forsaken:
the Measure and the Method of Mutuality

And now I am going to show you a way that is greater than all of them. (1 Cor 12:31)

In the previous chapter, we concentrated our attention on the summit of divine revelation in the 'Book of Glory' of the gospel of John. There the twelve, and through them, the whole church are invited to eavesdrop on the conversation between the paschal Christ and the Father of Love. (Jn 17) This invitation has been there since the beginning. (1 Jn 1:1) However, in more recent times it has emerged with vigour: time is a prerequisite of 'realisation' and realisation is the very life of religion. This is not to say that what is essential and dynamic in revelation has been inconsequential over almost two millennia, or that the church can suffer any kind of deep amnesia. On the contrary, the 'catholic principle of exegesis' (Hans Küng) ensures the pervasive, if subtle, presence of the whole of scripture in the church's life and action throughout time, which in any case now belongs to the Risen Christ. In fact, it is the same Lord who explains the scriptures as the church pursues her holy journey along the roads of the world. (Lk 24:13-35)

Still, it is true today that the People of God are re-appropriating this portion of divine revelation with fresh vigour. There is a growing realisation that this is what the Holy Spirit is saying to the church in our times. (Rev 3:22) Thus the great Council is shot through with the notion of communion and unity and the 'new commandment.'[1] It is as if the experience of Pentecost in the

---

1. See Michel Vandeleene (ed), *Egli è vivo!*, Roma 2006 for an ecclesiology elaborated in terms of the Risen Lord present among those who live by the new commandment and so are united in his name. (Mt 18:20)

Acts of the Apostles, that 'Big Bang' at the birth of the church, is impacting the church afresh and becoming available to the church in ways that had been unforeseen. Our surprise and our joy are in direct proportion.

What is in that very short Word?
The last chapter highlighted the new commandment and, in the resulting analysis, mentioned the 'measure' of the mutual love taught by Jesus and required of his disciples if the world is to believe and the church is to be credible. Only love is credible, and not any love, but that which has the measure of the heart of Jesus who loved us and gave himself up for us (Gal 2:20), the just for the unjust, the holy for the sinners, the Lord for the slave (1 Pet 3:18). 'Love one another *as* I have loved you.' The apostles would recall seeing this incomparable 'love to the end' (Jn 13:1; 19:30) in the crucified Son. Somehow this love effectively draws down the life that is above, or rather, the living out of it locates the life of the Holy Trinity in our world, as an unmistakable sign of the risen Lord of history and a pointer to his presence in humankind.

In this chapter our aim will be to draw out the implications for daily life among Christians, in the church and in society, of this revealed measure and method of mutuality. Our immediate object will be to focus on how that 'as' of the New Commandment is both the measure and the method of the mutual love that constitutes the life of the new and eternal covenant set up in the fullness of time and sealed in the shedding of the Blood of the New Covenant. (Gal 4:4; Rom 8:15; Heb 8:8-12; Jer 31:31; Lk 22:20; 1 Cor 11:26) The students of this 'as' are unanimous in stressing its centrality in understanding the content of the new commandment, which is itself the 'third commandment' after the first and the second which enjoin, respectively, the whole-hearted love of God and the love of neighbour 'as yourself'. (Mk 12:30; Rom 13:9) The Greek word *kathos* is stronger than other available prepositions. It 'does not indicate a simple comparison, an analogy that is more or less distant or a superficial similarity ... but a deep conformity, for the example of Jesus is also the norm of love and its foundation.' In fact, '*kathos* has a strong theological meaning: imitation and similarity, extension and assimilation: as the Father loves Jesus, so Jesus loves the believers (cf Jn 15:9; 17:23) and the believers must love one another with the same love (cf Jn 15:12) ... as the Father and the Son are one, the disciples must be one. (cf Jn17:21)'[2] The eternal sign or sacrament of that love is the crucified and forsaken Son: he loses everything for love of his Father and of us, except love.[3] Its measure is a mutual love that continues to love when all is lost and only pain and seeming disaster reign. Living this mutuality with this degree of gospel radicality seems to be what the Holy Spirit wants from the church in our times, as well as what the church owes to the human family in order to fulfil her age-old mission to the men and the women of our particular times. As the *Constitution on the Church in the Modern World, Gaudium et Spes*, states: 'The new command of love is the basic law of human perfection and hence of the world's transformation.'[4]

But what is the content of this intriguing little word? To answer that question, and so discover the authentic measure and method of the new commandment, it is necessary to study further the forsaken Jesus, for it is in him that the mysterious measure of his love is most fully manifest. His abandonment on the wood of the cross is the measure of his love for both his Father and for us, 'The world must know that I love the Father,' and 'As the Father has loved me, so have I loved you.' (Jn 15:9) It follows that it is necessary to see and discover in the forsaken Jesus the greatest possible revelation of the God who is love in himself and who is extreme in his love for us. (Eph 2:4) There are certain hermeneutical and theological hinterlands that need exploration in order to unpack the hidden treasures contained in the little word, *kathos*.

In the first instance, we shall look at the human and divine

---

2. C. Spicq, *Agape dans le Nouveau Testament, I*, Paris 1965, 161-174; 173, n 1.
3. See Heb 13:11-14.
4. *Gaudium et Spes*, 38.

tendency towards 'the more' and the 'greater' (the *magis* and the *maius*). The God of divine revelation and the scriptures is the God of the ever-more. Human beings, for their part, have always reached beyond themselves in search of something that is earlier, deeper or higher up on the ladder of reality. Then we shall cast an eye across some representative moments of spiritual insight occurring along the bimillennial journey of the church. These 'plunges' into the spiritual and lived history of the church will be a kind of verification of the previous insight, for these great 'charismatic' individuals loved to squander their lives, as it were, in the attempt to match the 'exceedingly great love of God' (Eph 2:4) which they perceive in revelation in virtue of the particular charism given to them. This will serve to throw light on the significance for spirituality of the discovery of Jesus Forsaken in the twentieth century. In a third moment, we will look at the striking entrance of the theme into post-war theology. Then we shall see the place this has come to occupy in the magisterium of Pope John Paul II. Finally, we will focus on a rather special experience of the spiritual and pastoral meaning of the 'as' in the New Commandment.

a. The Philosophical and Theological Background

As the philosopher Eric Voegelin has perceptively remarked, the constant of all cultures, paleolithic, mezzolithic, neolithic and historical, is the search for the ground.[5] So much is this the case that one could legitimately formulate the principle that the human being cannot be oneself except in the measure in which one reaches beyond oneself immeasurably. To be a human being is to be thrown beyond oneself. It is enough to think of some sample witnesses in support of the contention.

In the Neolithic Age there is the outstanding Irish example of the Boyne valley *tumuli*.[6] Here the great tumulus of Newgrange, constructed about 3200 BC, is so designed that on the morning of the Winter solstice, when there is least light in the northern

---

5. See Eric Voegelin, *Conversations with Eric Voegelin*, Montreal 1980.
6. Brendan M. Purcell, *The Drama of Humanity*, Frankfurt 1996, 56-74.

hemisphere, the sunlight makes its way down a long tumulus to a cruciform end where it illumines the ashes of the dead in three great quairns, and then floodlights the 'dome' of the passageway with the most amazingly brilliant light. Unless one wants to remain a rigid positivist, one has to read in this remarkable construction – itself older than the pyramids – a cry expressed in stone, circles and cross-lines from our ancient ancestors on this island for contact with the Light that conquers the darkness of the cosmos, and with the Life that is stronger than the death that pervasively pierces all human sides and wounds all hearts. One cannot forget the comment of G. K. Chesterton to the effect that cave men and women were artists.[7]

In the Golden Age of Greek philosophy, the same breakthrough occurred in terms of the clear differentiation between the Ground and everything else in a cosmos whose spokesperson could be man. Thus Bruno Schnell wrote of the 'discovery of mind' or *nous* in the Greek experience of philosophy as the constituent of humankind. The human being is a tension towards the very Ground of being, claimed Plato. The human soul desires and is in some way all things, adds Aristotle. Over one and a half millennia later, Thomas Aquinas enthusiastically agrees.[8] The human being is distinguished by the fact that s/he lives from and for and in that which is more than him/herself.

In the Christian context, this is memorably formulated by Augustine of Hippo when, at the outset of the *Confessions*, he writes: 'Our hearts are restless until they rest in You, O Lord.'[9] The thought of the whole tradition is concentrated provocatively in Blaise Pascal's adage, 'Man surpasses man infinitely.'[10] Commentators point out that the verb in the French has the twofold meaning of 'going beyond' and of 'colliding with'. The human destroys himself when he does not reach towards that

---

7. G. K. Chesterton, *The Everlasting Man*, New York 1955, 21-38.
8. St Thomas, '... *anima hominis sit omnia quodammodo,*' *Summa*, I, q. 80, a.1 c.
9. St Augustine, *Confessions*, I,1.
10. Blaise Pascal, '*L'homme passe infiniment l'homme*', *Pensées*, Fragm. 434, ed. Brunschvicg.

which is beyond him and which alone can fulfil him. By the same token, he fulfils himself when he aspires towards that which is beyond him and makes him strain forward.

It is perhaps permissible to see in the famous principle of St Anselm (1033-1109) that God is the 'that greater than which nothing can be thought'[11] a manifestation of the same insight. There resides in the deeper soul of the human being a longing for that which will always be greater than what we can manage to say, think or attain. Anselm explains: 'I can think of something that cannot be thought not to exist, and that is greater than what can be thought not to exist.' And it is precisely this quality of being always greater, and the fact that the human being is conscious thereof, that constitutes both the human mystery and the human drama.[12]

Even the dramatic rise of atheism does not negate this awareness: it may be pronounced nugatory as Nietzsche did, or diversionary and distracting as Marx did, or even deceitful as Freud did. Still, it returns inevitably and in surprising guises. Can one reverse the tide, or change the direction of the wind, or prevent the arrival of springtime? Any one of these might be achieved ere one can abolish this self-constituting thrust of *homo sapiens*.[13] And even if one were to attempt reversing the tide, would not the result be either a monster wave in nature or else a shameful defeat of an even more shocking presumption?

The question inevitably and universally, albeit with different emphases, arises, *where* is this Greater Reality, and *how* does one reach it? For as long as *homo sapiens* exists, this will remain the

---

11. St Anselm, *'id quo maius cogitari nequit' Proslogion*, cap. 2; see the even stronger formulation of this insight, 'One can think of something which cannot be thought not to exist, and that is greater than that which can be thought not to exist.'
12. This author cannot pass over the impact made upon the seventeen-year-old by Robert Louis Stevenson's essay 'Aes triplex' and its principle: 'It is better to lose health like a spendthrift than to waste it like a miser.' The ultimate question is perhaps, What constitutes that for which it makes sense to lose one's life like a spendthrift?
13. See C. S. Lewis, *The Abolition of Man*, Glasgow 1978, *passim*.

ineradicable hunger of the human heart. This, in fact, is the defining dimension of our humanity.

Now when one turns to the New Testament, one finds that it speaks of a great fact, namely, that God has loved us 'to the end.' (Jn 13:1) The Johannine corpus in particular stresses this fact. Jesus underlines the maximality of this love, '*Greater* love than this no one has than that he lay down his life for his friends.' (Jn 15:3) As the Saviour dies on the cross, his last word according to John is, 'It is finished.'[14] The greatest love is fulfilled. The God and Father of Jesus has shone into the deepest darkness. (1:9) Here is the greatest love, in fact a love greater than all other loves. This is the core of the message. Now the quest of humankind for the greater is in fact the quest for *this* ever-greater love that is revealed in the event of Jesus Christ.

Other 'layers' of the New Testament adopt the same posture. If one takes St Paul, for instance, it is enough to open the Letter to the Romans. The central portion of the letter, chapters five to eight, is a sustained exposition and meditation on the love of God shown in Christ and 'poured into our hearts by the Holy Spirit which has been given to us.' (5:5) In 8:32, perhaps the most audacious verse of the New Testament, he writes: 'Since God did not spare his own Son, but delivered him up for us all, will he not give us all things with him?' The longing for the greatest, the first and the ultimate on the human side is addressed by this love made known to us in Christ Jesus, our Lord. He manifests, makes present and communicates the knowledge of a love that is beyond all knowing. (Eph 3:19) This love 'drove' him, so to speak, to identify with his opposites, sin and damnation, out of love for the sinners and the damned (2 Cor 5:21 and Gal 3:14). In so doing he 'realigns' all of reality in a new rapport. Nothing, therefore, can separate us from the love of God. (Rom 8:35) On the contrary, 'all things belong to you, and you belong to Christ, and Christ belongs to God.' (1 Cor 3:22-23)

In the synoptic gospels, to investigate another layer of the

---

14. See Michael Mullins, *John*, Dublin 2003, 389 and Carlo M. Martini, *Il caso serio della fede*, Casale Monferrato 2002, 20-22, 169-170.

New Testament, one encounters the frequent strife among the disciples and the twelve for the first place. Perhaps one episode is enough to highlight the point. In Mark chapters nine and ten there is the debate among the twelve as to who was the greatest. The human being cannot *not* seek to be great and so to be associated with what is great, at least as he perceives it. However, Jesus reacts very vigorously to their actual identification of this greatness: he takes the 'little child' in his arms and places him among them to show that this is the greatest reality. (9:33-37; 10:35-45) Jesus does not deny at all the aspiration to greatness: he identifies its whereabouts and its character. The greatest reality is to serve out of love, to make oneself little out of generosity. Service, goodness and the gift of self constitute the Greatest Good. 'The true orientation towards the maximum is the orientation towards the minimum, towards that self-emptying where it becomes visible what God is – love. The fact that the human being seeks after that which is not himself but which is infinitely greater, is a reflection of the God who transcends himself and gives himself in a love greater than which none greater can be thought.'[15]

In the First Letter of St John, the logical implication of all this is identified: the human being must believe in this love which surpasses all knowing. Communicating the faith-experience of the Johannine community, the letter defines faith in this remarkable formula: 'We have believed in the love God has for us.' (4:16) Here one meets with the experience of an early Christian community sublimely expressed. It combines 'the faith by which' (*fides qua*) we accept with the love that first loved us (*fides quae*: 4:19). There is not in the whole of the New Testament a more theologically precise or simpler statement of the nature of Christian faith. The content of faith is 'God's love for us when he sent his Son to be the sacrifice that takes our sins away' (4:10), and the act of faith is already a participation in this same love, for, as St Thomas Aquinas so vividly saw, 'the act of faith does

---

15. Klaus Hemmerle, *Wegmarken der Einheit* in *Wie Glauben im Leben geht*, Munich 1995, 224.

not stop at the words but reaches the thing itself.'[16] That faith fulfils man's search for the greatest reality by identifying the 'greatest love' and then linking with that same love.

b. Sample Plunges into our Spiritual History

It is enough to survey briefly, in the time of the church, some representative moments when the kenotic love of God was perceived and lived in a manner that brought 'the gospel that God promised long ago' (Rom 1:2) alive with new vigour. Church history points out a golden thread of such experiences travelling across the centuries. Thus Ignatius of Antioch, who is martyred in the Colosseum about 110 AD, wishes to be nothing but 'an imitator of the sufferings of my God', to be 'ground like flour in order to become the Eucharist of Christ', for it is then that he will be truly a man.[17] Origen of Alexandria (256 AD), convinced that the eternal Son has been from all eternity overcome by the 'the passion of his charity' for the plight of humankind, could write: 'First he suffered, and then he descended and took on visible form. What sort of suffering was it that he underwent for our sake? The suffering of love. And the Father himself, the Lord of all, who is *longsuffering and rich in mercy* (Psalm 102:8) [103] – and compassion – does he not suffer as well in some respect? Or do you not know that when he dealt with human affairs he underwent human suffering? For *the Lord your God has taken your ways upon himself, just as a man carries his son* (Deut 1:31). God thus takes our ways upon himself, just as the Son of God bears our suffering.'[18] Little wonder, then, that Origen walked among his contemporaries in third-century Alexandria with the admonition-cry, 'Wake up to the love that sleeps within you.'

Augustine, the man that could not have rested content with

---

16. St Thomas, *Summa*, II-II, q.1, a.2 ad 2.

17. Ignatius of Antioch, *To the Romans*, 4.

18. Origen, *Homily on Ezechiel, 6.6: Sources Chrètiennes* 352, 22. Henri de Lubac sees this text of the great Alexandrine as 'no doubt one of his most beautiful pages, both his most human and his most Christian,' *Histoire et Esprit. L'intelligence de l'Ecriture d'après Origene*, Paris 1950, 241.

merely human love (John Henry Newman), and fascinated by
the eternal love that is the Trinity, asks the question, 'What do I
love when I love God? Do I not love Love?'[19] This Love loved us
first, and in loving us 'did not leave us as he found us. On the
contrary he made us beautiful ... for love is the beauty of the
soul.'[20] Through his acute and perceptive analysis of mutual
love, on whatever level it occurred, Augustine detected, as we
have seen in chapter ten, the reflection of that Love that is above,
the love of God the Holy Trinity. Here one locates that cry of St
Francis of Assisi (1226 AD) and his 'complaint' about the world:
'Love is not loved.' Hopkins captures something of the experience and insight of Francis in these lines:

> Joy fall to thee, father Francis,
> Drawn to the Life that died;
> With the gnarls of the nails in thee, niche of the lance,
> his
> Lovescape crucified.[21]

The crucified Son gathers all into the landscape that embraces all, unites all and can have only one possible name, Jesus
and he crucified, much like Paul. (1 Cor 1-2; 2 Cor 3-4) In his own
protest, Francis gave an example of gospel living that spread
around him a life that attracted and converted many to the kingdom of God.

In the motto of St Ignatius of Loyola (1555 AD), 'For the
greater glory of God,' one encounters that 'ever more' which the
human being seeks without resting and which God offers with a
boundlessness that shocks. In the School of Carmel, one encounters the contemplation of this crucified and glorified love in the
Spanish mystics, Teresa of Avila and John of the Cross. The latter puts it like this:

---

19. St Augustine, *De trinitate*, IX, 2.
20. *Idem, In I Joannem*, IX, 9.
21. Gerard Manley Hopkins, 'The Wreck of the Deutschland,' in *Poems
and Prose*, London 1953, 20: see Hans Urs von Balthasar's selection and
presentation of the theology of Hopkins as one of the eleven instances
of 'epoch-making theology' in the past two millennia, *The Glory of the
Lord, vol III, Lay Styles*, Edinburgh 1986, 353-399.

My Beloved, the mountains,
And lonely wooded valleys,
Strange islands,
And resounding rivers,
The whistling of love-stirring breezes.[22]

And is it not true that the great mystics of the Holy Eucharist
and of the Sacred Heart, Juliana of Luettich and Margaret Mary
Alacoque and Gertrude of Eisleben and Matt Talbot, all saw in
divine revelation the face of a love that enraptures, a love that is
pierced to heal all humankind and that seeks no authority except the authority of forgiving and self-consuming love, fire that
must be cast over the earth? At the beginning of the last century,
Charles de Foucauld (1916) noticed that 'Jesus had taken the last
place so perfectly that no one could ever take it away from him.'
That meant for Charles the mystery of Nazareth and the
abysmal humility of the eucharist: Charles desired only one
thing – to 'correspond' and to 'correlate' with so great a love.
The resultant desire drove him to live among and for his Muslim
brothers and sisters, together 'lost' among the eternal sand
dunes of the Sahara, an icon, prophetically, of the inter-religious
dialogue signalled at the Council and now getting underway.

And then there is Thérèse of Lisieux (1897 AD). Aware that we
have only one life, she desired to live it well, indeed to attain the
highest possible goal. Her 'desires' to make the living of life worth-
while to the greatest possible degree tormented her to the point of
despair. Desiring to be a missionary, a martyr, a teacher and
preacher of the gospel, a priest, she opened the First Letter to the
Corinthians. There the Word of God showed her 'the way that is
better than all' (1 Cor 12:31). She came to understand that love ensouls all missions in the Church. This love is their motor force and
highest common factor. The insight struck her with the power of a
tornado, 'I will *be* love in the heart of the Church, my mother!'[23]

---

22. St John of the Cross, *The Spiritual Canticle*, 14.
23. St Thérèse of Lisieux, Roman Breviary, Reading for Feast, first
October; see Hans Urs von Balthasar, *Two Sisters in the Spirit: Thérèse of
Lisieux and Elizabeth of the Trinity*, San Francisco 1992.

That is the greatest of all vocations. It is the spark that ignites all others, sustains them and makes them bear fruit. She had discovered the secret, the secret of becoming love, and, through love, of being All, the Greatest by participation.[24] The church has discerned in her insight the qualification for declaring her the thirty-third Doctor of the Church.

This all too brief a listing of key discoveries of treasures contained in the 'unfathomable riches of Christ' (Eph 3:8) attempts to put flesh and blood on a guiding insight, namely, that the human being can only find life when there is something for which it is unconditionally and absolutely meaningful to live and to die, and that the Absolute, for his part, has spoken: 'Yes, here I am. Here I am in the form that makes me most like you and for you, though it is impossible for me. But love for you made me do it. This love for you turned me against my own justice.' One notices, besides, that these samples demonstrate a definite correlation between the difficulties of an age and the particular discovery of an aspect of divine revelation that makes up for the deficit in such a way as to open up new vistas for theology and faith-life. Perhaps love for the crucified and forsaken Son-made-man responds best to the faith-deficit and culture-deficit of our era?

c. The Greatest Discovery of the Twentieth Century?
The twentieth century has seen enormous scientific and technological progress. It is enough to think that it is only shortly over one hundred years since the Wright brothers flew the first aeroplane. In the meantime we have walked on the moon and begun the exploration of space. The enormous benefits of medicine, communications and education have rendered human life more wholesome and full. The *Pastoral Constitution on the Church in the Modern World* identified this progress as one of the great signs of the times. It has had an enormous impact on humanity's self-understanding.

---

24. See St John of the Cross, *The Ascent of Mount Carmel*, book II, chapter 22.

The same century, however, has also witnessed wars on a scale never known before. Enormous loss of life resulted as if to verify Dostoyevsky's diagnosis, made towards the end of the previous century, that if God did not exist, everything would be permissible. The nineteenth century invented ideology to justify the systematically efficient slaughter of millions of innocent men, women and children, for, in the words of another great Russian, '... there is a disaster which is already very much with us ... the calamity of an autonomous, irreligious humanistic consciousness. It has made man the measure of all things on earth – imperfect man who is never free of pride, self-interest, envy, vanity and dozens of other defects.'[25]

It is legitimate to read modernity as the exaltation of one component of reality to the level of being the ultimate organising core of all reality. The result was a sequence of 're-divinisations.' Marxism 'divinised' the working classes as the messianic future of the world. Nietzsche divinised the will-to-power as the organising centre of reality. Freud divinised the unbridled will-to-pleasure as the constituent of human existence. The result of this process, so perceptively investigated by Eric Voegelin,[26] was the phenomenon of the ideologies. These great ideologies have seen a pattern of attempted implementation followed by massive 'prophetical disappointments'. They have led to a landscape of nihilism. Nihilism, in fact, is the outcome of these experiments with its central dogma that man is a freedom *from* everything but a freedom *for nothing*, since there is nothing either above or in front. The climate that results is that of indifference and 'exile' which becomes real when there is no more nostalgia for the fatherland.

However, these experiments with reality have also occasioned, and most paradoxically, a new search for God. Understandably this has to be a search *de profundis*, 'out of the depths'. That search, however, cannot be for any kind of God but only the God

25. Alexander Solzhenitsyn, *Alexander Solzhenitsyn Speaks to the West*, London 1978, 99.
26. Eric Voegelin, *The New Science of Politics*, Chicago and London 1952.

who is revealed at the summit of his loving us to be without God, yes, the God who cries out to God in solidarity with all the god-forsaken, 'My God, my God, why have you forsaken me?' (Mk 15:34; Mt 27:46)

When the Second World War concluded in 1945, leaving behind its *univers concentrationnaire* with its millions of murdered innocents, the cry went up everywhere, Can we speak of God after Auschwitz? If we can, what kind of God has it to be? It cannot be the God of Natural Theology, 'the God of the philosophers' (Pascal), nor the God of the Enlightenment. The first lives at the cold summit of reality as the Unmoved Mover (Aristotle) or the First Cause or as the conclusion of a syllogism, in metaphysical detachment from the affairs of humankind. The second knows nothing of the God of Abraham committing himself to a universal history for a universal humanity, a God who hears the cry of his people (Exodus 3:7; Ps 145:18), who is kind, full of compassion and rich in mercy to all who call upon him (Ps 83). The third, the God of the Enlightenment, is banished to the realm of irrelevance, since the Enligtenment forced this God to abdicate responsibility for the creation which he has made and to live in infinite apartness from his own handiwork.

The apocalyptic wars of the last century hastened the spread of a practical atheism: people began to live *'etiam si Deus non daretur,'* as if God did not exist.[27] The descent into the abyss had begun.[28] The cry of Nietzsche's madman rang out across the market places of Europe: 'God is dead.'[29] As heard by the Fathers assembled for the Second Vatican Council (1962-1965), that cry pierced to the heart. A pope commissions the theologians of the Jesuit Order to address 'the drama of atheist humanism,'[30] while the Council itself wonders as to the responsibility of believers themselves for the advent and diffusion of practical

27. Hugo Grotius, *De iure belli et pacis*, Prolegomena 11.
28. See David Walsh, *After Ideology*, New York 1990, 58-75.
29. Friederich Nietzsche, *The Happy Science*, 125.
30. This is the title of Henri de Lubac's masterly study of atheism, San Francisco 1995; see Martin Henry, *On not Understanding God*, Dublin 1996.

atheism.[31] If the lifestyle of Christians witnesses to a God who is not the God of Jesus Christ, a God who freely, radically and lovingly involves himself in the human drama 'to the end', have we believers not perhaps misrepresented the God who chose the way of the cross (Mk 8:31-38)? Perhaps believers themselves must shoulder some of the blame for the God-forsakenness of many of our contemporaries in not manifesting the true face of God.[32] Has the God of Jesus Christ been a God who stops gaps, a *Deus ex machina*, a God who guarantees personal peace and protection against the slings and arrows of outrageous fortune? Is he not rather the God who cried out in the anguish of an infinite divine-human forsakenness because he had taken to himself, not only our human nature, but also our *human condition* (St Leo the Great)?

There is also a certain kind of 'pre-understanding', the fruit of a form of heuristic knowing by which that which is still to be appropriated in the riches of divine revelation[33] can be named. Just as the feminine genius of a Thérèse of Lisieux succeeded both in naming ('I wanted to do something great') and locating ('Delirious with joy, I cried out, "I have found my way: I shall be love at the heart of the Church, my mother"') the Fullness and the Greatest in the ordinary events of each day, thereby opening up to masses of believers her great 'Little Way' to live the adventure of the gospel,[34] so too these theologians and charismatic Christians made an epoch-making discovery in the cry of god-forsakenness of the dying God-Man, 'My God, my God, why have you forsaken me?' (Mk 15:34; Mt 27:46) *Ecce Deus! Ecce Homo!* Behold your God! Behold yourself!

In the God-Man obedient unto death on the cross, going forth to die outside the city (Heb 13:13) and therefore accursed with

---

31. *Gaudium et spes*, 19: see International Theological Commission, *Memory and Reconciliation. The Church confronts the Sins of the Past*, London 2000.
32. See *Gaudium et spes*, 19.
33. See *Dei Verbum*, 8.
34. Thérèse of Lisieux, *Manuscript B, 3v: Oeuvres completes*, Paris 1996, 226.

the accursed, become sin with the sinners (2 Cor 5:21) one hears two voices: with one ear one hears the voice of an infinite suffering, with the other ear one hears the voice of an infinite love, for it is nothing less than the love that is God (1 Jn 4:8, 16). The very question of the suffering of the innocent that made the God of Natural Theology, of the philosophers and of the Enlightenment simply 'incredible', gropes towards a sea of infinity, mysterious with the suffering that is born out of an ever greater love. Paradoxically, the very question of classical theodicy becomes the challenge 'not to think less, but the provocation to think more, indeed to think differently.'[35] Evil and suffering become the very context, indeed the grammar, of God's discourse to us in his Son made flesh and forsaken on the wood of the cross, since the Son interprets himself for us in this most scandalous manner: 'When you have lifted up the Son of Man, then you will know that I am he.' (Jn 8:28) Only this Son crucified and forsaken 'says' God to us adequately. In this Son abandoned out of love for us, the Father 'says' himself and 'speaks' himself in a manner greater than which none can be thought. Conversely, it is only he who lifts us, *precisely as we are*, with him and in him towards that same Father.

This sets up the context for a fresh reading of the New Testament. The dramatic circumstances obtaining at the end of the second millennium have generated a new hermeneutic for that reading. The history of theology over the whole course of Christian history disposes us in fact to look out for a new hermeneutic. Such a hermeneutic will enable us to discern undiscovered deposits in the very text of divine revelation. No one finds answers to the questions he or she has not asked. This is in fact what happened: in the Orthodox, Protestant and Catholic churches, theologians and theologies emerge to express the 'new things' (Is 43:19) always present but undetected until now in the Master's storehouse. In the Orthodox world it is

---

35. Paul Ricoeur, *Le mal. Le defi à la philosophie et à la théologie*, Genève 1986.

enough to mention Sergei Bulgakov,[36] in the Lutheran world, Jürgen Moltmann,[37] and in the Catholic world, Hans Urs von Balthasar.[38]

The thought of these three thinkers has been an extraordinary enrichment of faith and faith-life in their respective churches. It has also helped to initiate a rich dialogue between these same churches. This fact points towards the fruitfulness of the God-forsaken Son who is the Lord of glory (1 Cor 2:8). It strongly hints at the unifying energy of the crucified and abandoned Christ for 'the gathering of the scattered' (Jn 11:52) and the restoration of unity. The conviction of the Apostle of the Gentiles that 'the word of the cross' (1 Cor 1:18) is the wisdom of God for all who are on the way to salvation is achieving a new and surprising currency.

d. The entry of the theme into the magisterium of John Paul II
The theme of Jesus crucified and forsaken has entered profoundly into the magisterium of Pope John Paul II. In an Apostolic Letter on the theme of suffering, *Salvifici Doloris*, written in 1984, he highlights the fact of the forsakenness of the Redeemer on the wood of the cross. Daringly, he focuses our minds on this moment in the Saviour's life, having led us there with careful steps. Referring to the cry of abandonment on the cross, the pope writes: 'One can say that these words on abandonment are born at the level of that inseparable union of the Son with the Father, and are born because the Father "laid on him the iniquity of us all."(Is 53:6) They also foreshadow the words of St Paul: "For our sake he made him to be sin who knew no sin."(2 Cor 5:21) Together with this horrible weight, *encompassing the "entire" evil of the turning away from God* which is contained in sin, Christ, through the divine depth of his filial union with the Father, perceives in a humanly inexpressible way *this suffering which is the separation*, the rejection *by the Father*, the es-

---

36. See especially his magisterial *The Lamb of God* , 1933.
37. Jürgen Moltmann, *The Crucified God*, London 1974.
38. Hans Urs von Balthasar, *Mysterium Paschale*, Edinburgh 1990.

trangement from God.'[39] Already in the long encyclical on the Holy Spirit, *Dominum et Vivificantem*, he wrote: 'The concept of God as a necessarily most perfect Being definitely excludes from God all suffering that derives from deficiencies or wounds ... But the Sacred Book speaks to us of a Father who feels compassion for men and women, almost sharing in their suffering.'[40]

However, it is in the encyclical on faith and reason, *Fides et Ratio*, that he formally puts the theme of the God-forsakenness of the Lord on the theological agenda. There he writes: 'The preaching of Christ crucified and risen is the reef upon which the link between faith and philosophy can break up, but it is also the reef upon which the two can set forth upon the boundless ocean of truth. Here we see not only the border between reason and faith, but also the space where the two may meet.'[41] As if captivated by the theme, he returns to it again in his inspiring Apostolic Letter for the third millennium, *Novo Millennio Ineunte*. There he explains that 'Jesus' cry on the cross ... is not the cry of anguish of a man without hope, but the prayer of the Son who offers his life to the Father in love, for the salvation of all. At the very moment when he identifies with our sin, "abandoned" by the Father, he "abandons" himself into the hands of the Father.'[42]

The theme of Jesus crucified and forsaken precedes that of the 'spirituality of communion' which the pope declares to be the imperative for the life of the church as she moves on her pilgrim way into the third millennium. 'To make the church *the home and the school of communion*: that is the great challenge facing us in the millennium which is now beginning, if we wish to be faithful to God's plan and respond to the world's deepest yearnings.' This is the foundation, the indispensable foundation, for education and for all the pastoral projects of the church in the third millennium. 'Unless we follow this spiritual path, external

---

39. Pope John Paul II, *Salvifici Doloris*, 18

40. *Idem, Dominum et Vivificantem*, 93.

41. *Idem, Fides et Ratio*, 23.

42. *Idem, Novo Millennio Ineunte*, 26.

structures of communion will serve very little purpose. They would become mechanisms without a soul, "masks" of communion rather than its means of expression and growth.'[43] The precedence of communion over activity, of being over acting, stands out.

'Love one another as I have loved you' (Jn 13:34; 15:12)
Jesus crucified and forsaken, then, is the measure, the method and the 'energy' of the new commandment. As measure, he indicates how extreme and total is the love required of Christians. It is after all the love that comes from the bosom of the Trinity and that Jesus 'prolongs' towards the disciples. By definition such a love finds its perfection in the extreme, not in the mean, but in 'the greatest of these'. (1 Cor 13:13)

Jesus crucified and forsaken also shows the 'method' by which it can be lived. He lives the reality of the other to the point where he carries the whole 'baggage' of the other. Jesus lives the other, entering into the abyss of his life. The law of his existence consisted in carrying the others and the others' burdens. (Gal 6:2) Our age is characterised by loneliness, meaninglessness, abandonment and anguish. Jesus is the 'method' by which one can live these states *in others and in oneself*. 'The image of Jesus spread out between earth and heaven and experiencing abandonment by the Father and by human beings is the ultimate *Ecce Homo* for the men and the women of today. He is their mirror. However, he is a mirror in which men and women can look not only upon themselves but also upon the one who infinitely transcends them, the God who out of love throws himself into their situation. Their own loneliness and abandonment become the very place in which the love of God encounters them.'[44] *Ecce Deus!* Behold your God!

The one who endures the abandonment 'for us and for our salvation' is also the source of our strength, for we need great

---

43. *Ibid.*, 43.
44. Klaus Hemmerle, *Wegmarken der Einheit*, in *Wie Glauben im Leben geht*, Munich 1995, 229.

energy to live the other as another me. In fact, this is only possible by an inner revolution of mind. (Rom 12:2) He is in us as 'the hope of glory,' (Col 1:27) indeed, but his grace has to enable and to energise our hearts of stone with the warm love that his God-forsakenness both shows and communicates. Else, how can we 'see the other always as better' (Phil 2:3), worthy of our dedication simply as 'the brother for whom Christ died'? (1 Cor 8:11) In the Father-forsakenness of the enfleshed Son there is a hidden resource. It is hidden in fact since the foundation of the church. Because it is hidden, it is only gradually discerned. This 'resource' functions to expand our hearts to the measure of his heart so that Christians begin to love each other in the measure he has first loved them, in each others' abandonments and to the point of mutual abandonment.

The new commandment is lived only when at least two people live in the fashion just described. Such Christians live the authentic mutuality that is both the necessary presupposition of the new commandment and its content. It is this degree of love leading to such a mutuality that meets the criterion for the unambiguous living out of the new commandment as the 'dying wish' of the Redeemer. Such people, be they the mere evangelical two or three gathered in the Lord's name (Mt 18:20) or more, radiate the kingdom of God the Holy Trinity in the world. They do so wherever they are found. All will recognise them as the disciples of Christ. (Jn 13:35; 15:12; 17:21)

Today many seem quite incapable of finding God 'vertically' as it were. The Lord of History, however, has opened up this 'new way' (1 Cor 12:31) for his church, a way that is 'lived' horizontally. This way comes into being when Christians live the new commandment of Jesus as the love that mutually honours and serves and carries the burdens of the others in fulfilment of the Law of Christ. (Gal 6:2) Perhaps this is the reason why the Council stresses that it is the new commandment which is the law of development of the human family.[45]

---

45. See *Gaudium et spes*, 38.

Forgotten Truths: the Loss

Divine revelation contains the hidden mysteries of God the Holy Trinity but communicates them to humankind and to creation so that we may participate in the life of the same Holy Trinity. By definition these 'unfathomable riches' (Eph 3:8) not only exceed our understanding,[46] they also are *un embarrass des richesses*. That embarrassment, however, has been added to by a further factor: great dimensions of the faith given once for all to the saints (Jude 3) fade from view. Once out of sight they are quickly out of mind. In a particular way, this has happened with the christological substance of the faith – the necessary dogmas have indeed been taught, and in the very teeth of biting subtle heresy – but whole fragments have gone missing from the consciousness of Christians over the Christian centuries. This may go a long ways towards explaining the possible initial 'strangeness' of both the subject and the argument of this chapter. In any case, it does require us to look for a short while at the way in which the christological substance was damaged by such amnesia.

Many authors have drawn attention to the fact that believers have failed to notice the riches of the events of the incarnation and the paschal mystery after the great early Councils. In a particular way, the teaching of the Council of Chalcedon, or rather the subsequent employment of its creed, tended to separate the mystery of Christ from its engendering and engrossing setting in the pages of the New Testament. The formula of the Council indeed protected the truth of Christ in the unity of his divine Person as the co-eternal Son and in the twofold of his natures as truly God and truly man. Christ was 'consubstantial with the Father in divinity' and 'consubstantial with us in humanity'. 'It said in Hellenistic terms something quite unHellenistic.'[47]

However, its teaching failed to become what it set out to be – a vital formula. And no formula, however venerable, can save

---

46. First Vatican Council, *Constitutio dogmatica de fide catholica*, chapter 4 in Tanner, II, 808-809.
47. See Walter Kasper, 'Einer aus der Trinität', in *Theologie und Kirche*, Mainz 1987, 217-227; the formula 'One of the Three' is from the Fifth Ecumenical Council at Constantinople in 553 AD.

us. The formula began to encapsulate and hide away the Person of the eternal Son living a truly human life because 'like us in all things except sin'. (Heb 4:15) The result has been a serious impoverishment in our understanding of what happened in the event of Christ, particularly in the paschal mystery of his passion, death, resurrection and sending of the Holy Spirit.[48] It is useful to name some aspects of this impoverishment.

The incarnation became the focus of attention. It was cut off, as it were, from the whole unfolding drama of the God-Man's life. The point in time when the Timeless intersected with time becomes the only point on which the mind is made to concentrate. The gospels and the letters, however, have an entirely different focus, being almost 'passion narratives with long introductions.' (Kähler) In the Philippians' hymn (2:6-11), to take but one example of pre-Pauline christology, there is the dramatic follow-through from the *kenosis* of incarnation to the still greater *kenosis* of the cross. Irenaeus in fact wrote of 'the Son descending, becoming incarnate and descending even as far as death.'[49] And with this oversight there is a forgetting of the protological horizon of creation as well.

Chalcedon speaks of a double consubstantiality, with the Father in divinity but *with us in humanity*. After Chalcedon, however, the second 'being one with' is increasingly overlooked. Jesus' consubstantiality with us in humanity is gradually lost to view. The Christ of the gospels, who has compassion on the crowd and weeps over Jerusalem (Lk 19:41-44), will be passed over as if he has little or nothing to say to human history. His extreme solidarity with all men and women will disappear. The result is an unbridgeable distance between the enfleshed Son and men and women. Such a distance, however, runs contrary to the witness of the gospels to the Son of Man. It conflicts with the evangelical message that Jesus is the only way to the Father for all because he is ontologically one with the Father (Jn 14:6; 10:30) and *economically* one with every son and daughter of

---

48. See *Dei Verbum*, 4.
49. St Irenaeus, *Adversus Haereses*, III, 18, 1-2.

Adam. In that way it leads inevitably back to a *practical mono-physitism* which, paradoxically, had been rejected at Chalcedon.

This reduction of the mystery of Christ, thirdly, led to the loss of a great insight worked out by the Fathers of the East and the West, namely, that human beings are as 'many words in the One Word', 'ideas in the eternal Word' (Augustine and Maximus the Confessor). Christ is the eternal image and likeness of God. All men and women, as created in the image and the likeness of that God, find their centre and their meaning in him alone. As the one 'in whom and for whom all things in heaven and on earth were created' (Col 1:16; see Jn 1:3; Eph 1:4), he is the focal point of reality. According to the Fathers, it is not possible to understand Christianity at all outside this perspective. For Gregory of Nyssa, to speak of human individuals outside this unity of the many in the One is as gross as to speak of three 'Gods' in the Blessed Trinity.[50] St Cyril of Alexandria puts these words on the lips of Christ: 'By my flesh I have redeemed the flesh of all men. For in my death death will die, and fallen human nature will rise again with me.'[51]

The divine motivation of the incarnation emerges as a theme. However, the motive becomes almost exclusively hamartological. Christ became man to save us from sin. Of course, the texts in the New Testament are numerous in affirmation of this dimension. However, there are many other texts that highlight other vital perspectives. Thomas Aquinas clearly affirms that we should not place limits on 'the power of God, since he could have become incarnate also in the absence of sin.'[52]

The exclusive preoccupation with the incarnation and its metaphysics led, finally, to an overlooking of the role of Mary in the concrete event of Christ. This is more than strange, for only thirty years before Chalcedon, the Council of Ephesus had affirmed Mary to be *Theotokos*, the *Genetrix Dei*. To have left out

---

50. St Gregory of Nyssa, *De hominis opificio*, 8: PG 44, 185 B-D.
51. St Cyril of Alexandria, *Commentary of St John, IV*, 2 (Breviary, Easter 3, Sat).
52. St Thomas Aquinas, *Summa*, III, q.1, a.3 c; see Duns Scotus, *Reportatio Parisiensis*, in *III Sententiam*, d. 7, a.4.

this dimension was to have missed the dialogical principle that runs through divine revelation from beginning to end. Mary is the Omega-point in the dialogue of the God of Abraham with Israel. This makes Mary the dialogue-partner of God *par excellence* since she is the representative of Israel, the Daughter of Sion in person, when the God of Israel makes his final offer to humankind.[53] She is at the point where the First Covenant becomes the New and the synagogue passes over into the church.

Towards the Fullness of the Mystery

The Italian theologian, Piero Coda, states a principle that is vital in this context of retrieving lost dimensions of revelation. A solid and profound unitary vision of the creation-salvation mystery of Christ is to be aimed at and as far as possible articulated.[54] This approach connects at once the pre-existent Logos with the incarnate Logos who then gathers up the cosmos, humankind and history through the Holy Spirit into eschatological fullness when God will be all in all. (1 Cor 15:28) Such a perspective connects protology, incarnation and eschatology, because it takes seriously what the scriptures love to call 'the mystery of Christ'. (Rom 16:25; 1 Cor 2:7; Eph 3:10; Col 1:26-7; 2:2-3) The revelation of this mystery is what was going forward in history, in the patriarchs and the prophets, until in Jesus Christ it is fulfilled, manifested and communicated.

This mystery consists in the plan of God the Holy Trinity to gather up (*anakephalaiosis*) all things in heaven and on earth – the whole of creation – through Christ, having 'made peace by the blood of his cross'. Christ in fact is the agent and the instrument of the eternal purpose of God (Eph 3:11), the plan that had been hidden for all ages in the God who had created all things. (Eph 3:9) Christ is no afterthought of God but his very forethought, the one through whom the Father knew and created all reality before re-creating it by his blood and glorifying it by his resur-

---

53. See St Thomas Aquinas, *Summa*, III, q.30, a.1 where he speaks of the *'consensus virginis loco totius humanae naturae.'*
54. Piero Coda, *Il logos e il nulla*, Roma, 2003, 206-7.

rection and the outpouring of the holy Spirit. (Eph 1:6; Col 1:20) This fact is incomparably enunciated in Ephesians 2:10: 'We are what he has made us, created in Christ Jesus for good works, which God created beforehand to be our way of life.' (*NRSV*) As Teilhard de Chardin saw with such passionate clarity, Creation is finalised in Christ and for Christ and through Christ.[55]

This revealed perspective, so strongly present in the Pauline literature, is a dynamic one. It highlights not only the pre-existence of the Word and the dynamism of the Trinitarian life, but also the freely chosen project of the Trinity to create, redeem and glorify all creation. It was always the 'plan' and the 'will' of the Trinity to set up and conduct such a project outside. This is what the tradition calls the 'economy'.[56] At the centre of the economy is creation and its summit, Man, understood both collectively and individually, who is destined to be 'christened' along with creation in the event of the incarnation and the economy of the Logos and the Holy Spirit. This means that God has an expression of himself within himself, and another expression of himself outside, as it were. These two expressions exist without separation and without confusion, to use the language of Chalcedon. The economy, in other words, consists in the fullness of the mystery of Christ.

It is a serious distortion to relate the two 'expressions' in such fashion that God the Holy Trinity needs the project to become himself. Such a view introduces myth into God and breaks down the basic revelation that God is love to the point that they wish to scatter themselves. The greatness of Hegel consists in the attempt to rethink everything from the perspective of the Trinity. The dangerous weakness, however, is that he makes God dependent on his own creation. The infinite Spirit becomes Trinity in the final encounter with matter, humankind and history on Calvary – a speculative Good Friday.[57] Both Bonaventure

---

55. Pierre Teilhard de Chardin, *Le Milieu Divin*; see Henri de Lubac, *The Faith of Teilhard de Chardin*, London 1965, 'The cosmic Christ', 29-38.
56. See Henri de Lubac, *Catholicism*, London 1950, chapter 1: 'Dogma', 1-13.
57. See David Bentley Hart, *The Beauty of the Infinite*, Grand Rapids 2003, 38-40.

and Aquinas articulated the clear principle that creation and recreation, the economy, are an overflowing of God's goodness such that they ground the apostolic principle, 'God is love.' It is difficult to find a more succinct 'neighbour principle' to that principle than that 'the good scatters itself.'[58]

'As the Father has loved me, so have I loved you' (Jn 15:9)

The pronominal precision of the fourth gospel, to which we have already alluded, facilitates theological analysis of the most theological gospel and of the New Testament in general. The analysis we propose here is to take the two main clauses that constitute the sentence in reverse 'economical' order, and then, in the third place, to link them via the great little word 'as'. Thus we shall consider Jesus' own declaration, 'I have loved you', then his revelation, 'The Father has loved me', and, finally, the significance of the linking principle 'as' for the resulting under-standing and theology.

'I have loved you'

As the embodied revelation of the Father (Jn 1:14; 6:51; 1 Jn 1:1), the Son is the deed of love *par excellence*. Revelation operates, as we have seen, via 'words and deeds that are intrinsically con-nected'.[59] The infinite Word 'says' himself via the deed of loving us, namely, 'giving his life as a ransom for many'. (Mk 10:45) We need to enter into the infinite Word performing this infinite deed. The challenge, in other words, is to understand why and how the raising up of the Word made flesh on the wood of the cross shows that Jesus is the divine 'I am' (Jn 8:28), and becomes the magnetic centre drawing all into unity. (12:32; 17:21)

Jesus shows the truth which he is via the deed of the cross which occurs in the time of 'the hour'. (Jn 2:5) If he shows him-self, ours is the task to 'come and see'. (1:47) In Jesus we en-counter the one who concretely loves 'to the end' (13:1) and so shows a love that is always greater. This love is an absolute com-

---

58. St Thomas, '*Bonum est diffusivum sui*' in *Summa*, I, q.5, a.4 ad 2.
59. *Dei Verbum*, 2.

parative: never can a greater be encountered (Eph 3:19). As love
made flesh, Jesus wishes to mediate to us the life he had with the
Father before the creation of the world. This suggests that the
cipher of mediator is perhaps the key to that love that is the sig-
nature of his person and deeds and words. Jesus in fact is our
mediator with the Father and with one another. (Gal 3:28-29)

This theme stands out in the Letter to the Hebrews. Jesus has
introduced us into the life of God, taking us once and for all with
himself into the heavenly sanctuary. As such, Jesus is 'the mediator of a new covenant' (9:15) which is infinitely superior to the
previous one. (8:6) Experienced and tried in suffering (4:15-5:10),
he is still the eternal Son of God: indeed more, he is capable of
sympathising with us in all our sorrows because he has been
tested in every way as we are, though without sinning (4:15).

John puts it with incomparable brevity: 'The Word became
flesh.' (1:14) St Augustine comments elegantly on this text:
'Jesus is the Word with God, the flesh with us, and the Word
made flesh between us.'[60] Only by his ontological qualification
as both truly God and truly man, could he be their authentic
mediator. The fourth century Fathers derived two principles to
highlight the truth of this mediation: first, unless he is God, he is
not able to link humanity to the Creator; second, 'that which the
Son has not assumed he has not healed.'[61]

The resulting bond between God and man is not merely vertical. It is also horizontal. This is a perspective which we find extremely unfamiliar in contemporary culture. Yes, we accept that
the Word did indeed become flesh, 'taking on what he was not
and not losing what he is.' But what we find extremely difficult
is to understand how he thereby reached all men and women of
all times. Now both Greek philosophy and Old Testament revelation had principles that facilitated this understanding. In the
former, there was the insight that all the individuals were one

---

60. St Augustine, *De Genesi ad Litteram, VIII,* 32; see *Discourse* 47, 21 in
PL 38, 310.
61. Gregory Nazianzen, *Letter 101,* Library of Nicene and Post-Nicene
Fathers, VII, 440.

through sharing one and the same human nature. There was the breakthrough to universal humanity. When the eternal Son takes up this human nature he takes up in some way all the individuals who are one in that very nature. In assuming human nature, the Word assumes universal humanity. As for Israel, there was the manifest fact of 'corporate personality' by which an individual person might sum up the whole people, as, for instance, the king, the Daughter of Zion, the Suffering Servant of Yahweh. The fact that contemporary culture has lost this sense of solidarity makes these notions sound rather strange. Still, the reality revealed and symbolised in the pages of the New Testament does not disappear.

The great Russian Orthodox theologian, Sergei Bulgakov (1944), comments on this loss of substance as follows: 'The very putting of the question is tainted with individualism and legalism since it recognises only persons who are [as] separated and singularised ... However, the distinction of this kind between 'mine' and 'yours' is abolished by love, which over and above distinction also recognises the unity/identity of the I and the You. That which appears absurd to natural justice becomes natural to love. Above all, however, Christ is not in fact 'another' in relation to each human being, since the New Adam enfolds/embraces in his essence by nature and by the sympathy of his love every human individual. He is the universal man.'[62] Or as Hans Urs von Balthasar would state it, Jesus Christ is the Catholic, since as the New Adam he embraces all the sons and daughters of the First Adam and the First Eve in himself.[63] Through the double bond of shared nature and of love, the incarnate Word is one with every man and woman so that it is no gospel exaggeration whatsoever that Jesus should repeat: 'In so far as you did this to one of the least of these brothers of mine, you did it to me.' (Mt 25:40) This is the key to the teaching of the *Pastoral Constitution on the Church in the Modern World* when it

---

62. Sergei Bulgakov, *The Lamb of God*, London 1933, 431-2.
63. Hans Urs von Balthasar, 'Anspruch auf Katholizität' in *Pneuma und Institution*, Einsiedeln 1974, 61-116; also *Theodrama, III*, Milano, 218-221.

says, 'With his incarnation the Son of God has united himself in some way with every human being.' (22)

This vision of the love of the one mediator between God and Man (1 Tim 2:5) as just described is still static. It needs to unfold into the dynamic effects of such a divine and human solidarity. The first of these effects is that of the 'wondrous exchange' which the Fathers highlight. The Fathers love to draw out this dimension. Thus Irenaeus writes: 'The Son of God became the son of man so that the human being by uniting himself to the Word and so receiving the divine sonship, should become the Son of God.' In a word, 'The Son of God became what we are so that we might become what he is.'[64] The eternal Son descends into what is infinitely beneath him so that humankind, indeed the whole of history and the world itself, might be divinised by entering with him and through him into the life and communion that is the Trinity.

The Son of the Father, however, loved us in our sinful condition as separated and opposed to his Father and to one another. Here we meet a second effect, as it were, of the mediation of the Christ. St Gregory of Nazianzen writes these words: 'Christ takes me whole and entire within himself with all my misery in order to destroy in himself evil, like fire that dissolves in itself the wax.'[65] Blaise Pascal many centuries later puts it like this: 'The knowledge of God without that of man's misery causes pride. The knowledge of man's misery without that of God causes despair. The knowledge of Jesus Christ constitutes the middle cause, because in him we find both God and our misery.'[66]

On coming into our world and history by the way of incarnation and death on the Roman patibulum, the Son of God 'tasted' our human condition of suffering and sin and death (Heb), of sorrow and separation as no else ever could. In a particular way,

---

64. St Irenaeus, *Adversus Haereses*, III, 19, 1; V, *praefatio*; see the International Theological Commission, *Quaestiones selectae de Christologia, Enchiridion Vaticanum 7*, n. 683, '*Praeterea homo ad integrationem in Christo, et eo ipso in vitam trinitariam, creatus est.*'
65. St Gregory Nazianzen, *Oration* 30, 6: PG 36, 109.
66. Blaise Pascal, *Pensées*, 526, 527.

he descended into the situation engendered by our very revolt against God, itself the germ and the core of each and every sin. He is not only emptied out by assuming the condition of a creature, much more he is in a situation dominated by a disunity with the Creator, his Father, and between human beings. Like a virus infecting the good Creation of his Father, a creation grounded in himself – 'he holds all things in unity' (Col 1:17) – sin has acted as the power of disintegration. (Augustine) This is the creation he must love with a might greater than that of sin.

> O wisest Love! that flesh and blood
> Which did in Adam fail
> Should strive afresh against the foe,
> Should strive and should prevail. (John Henry Newman)

As the sinless one he alone knows the ugliness of the unlove at the dead heart of sin. As the innocent one he alone knows what it is to be burdened by the guilt of all of us (Is 53:6; 1 Pet 2:21). As the one for whom the very thought of evil is a sword penetrating his soul with unspeakable anguish, to be made into sin for us so that in him we could become the goodness of God (2 Cor 5:21) is an exchange that filled him with a pain that exceeds all our reckoning.[67]

The very purpose of the first *kenosis* is attained in the second where the way to the glory of the Father is opened up 'for us men and women and for our salvation'. It is here, in other words, that the Son becomes truly and fully man, an insight grasped by the early Colosseum martyr, Ignatius of Antioch: 'Only when I come thither shall I be truly a man. Leave me to imitate the Passion of my God.'[68] In the experience of the cross, the Word made flesh lives to the full the consequence of his incarnation as 'the *reductio ad hominem* of the Logos of God.' However, this very same *reductio* accomplishes his mission as

---

67. Some of Christ's greatest friends were graced with a certain participation in this anguish of the redeeming God-man, as, to name but a few, Catherine of Siena, the Curé of Ars, Padre Pio and Gemma Galgani.

68. Ignatius of Antioch, *Letter to the Romans*, 6.

'the *reductio ad Deum* of the man Jesus and, in him, of all and everything.'[69] Theologians from Thomas until Emile Mersch and Anselm Stolz speak variously of either 'an accidental hypostatic union' between humankind and Christ, or our being 'one mystical person in Christ'[70]

A young theologian identifies incisively the core of the anguish of the Redeemer as resulting from his entering through love for sinners – not for sin which he detests – into the situation brought about by sin: 'Jesus goes directly to the root. He does not involve himself in the transgression, which exists and is to be rejected, but he takes upon himself the situation of the absence of God which is the effect of each and every sin.'[71] As a father or mother, while hating the immorality indulged in by a prodigal child and now the cause of life-threatening disease, still suffers with and for that child, so too only more profoundly does the God of love enter the godforsakenness brought on by sin. Here we touch on the great theme of the second *kenosis* which we have already had occasion to consider. The result is that he puts light where there is the darkness of sin, hope where there is the despair of evil, freedom where there is only the slavery of sin, and beauty subverting the real ugliness of evil.

A third effect of the mediatorship of Christ now comes clearly into view, namely, the crucified and forsaken Christ as the one who is the ransom for our sins and who thereby transforms death into life, non-being into being, nothingness into fullness, and separation into fullness. It is enough to think of Jesus' intention 'to give his life as ransom for many'(Mk 10:45) or the statement in 1 Tim 2:6: 'the man Christ Jesus who has given his life as ransom for many.' Rather than a price to be paid to the Father – something that is infinitely grotesque and without any foundation whatsoever in the New Testament[72] – the ransom is an

---

69. Piero Coda, *Il Logos e il nulla*, Roma 2002, 208.
70. St Thomas, *De Veritate*, 29, 4; *Summa*, III, q.48, a.2, ad 1.
71. Hubertus Blaumeiser, '*Un mediatore che è nulla*' in *Nuova Umanità*, XX (1998/3-4), 396.
72. B. Sesboüé, *Gesù Cristo l'unico mediatore*, I, 170.

emptiness in us that has to be filled. A great contemporary Christian, Chiara Lubich, puts it in these terms: 'Having made himself sin and therefore disunity, individuality, Jesus as the abandoned one can be the partner also of the last sinner of the world, and can be separated from all, because he, as sin, is seen in all the sinners and all the sinners can see themselves in him.'[73]

When the New Testament speaks of 'ransom', 'expiation' or 'reparation' it is never to be understood as something to be paid to the Father by his incarnate Son. Such a conception of God owes more to mythology than it does to revelation. The Father and the Son 'conspire' together in the Holy Spirit for our salvation. Olivier Clément states the case very well when he writes: 'The condition of death brought about by sin is not a punishment, or is at the most a self-inflicted one which God turns into a cure. Death is the result of rejecting the living God, excluding the Creator from his creation. But God was to take flesh and die, in order to fill death itself with his love and turn it into resurrection for the human race. An anthropology which embraces such a notion of sin will deal with good and evil in terms not of moral value, but of being and non-being, life and death, communion and separation, disease and healing.'[74] The fifth-century Father, Peter Chrysologus, has the crucified Christ address the Christian in these words: 'See, I return good for evil, love for injuries, and for deeper wounds a deeper love.'[75]

Jesus, then, becomes a nothingness, a nothingness of love. This is what leads to the abandonment, that hidden wound that theologians have recently discovered, that saints have lived by, and that the poor in spirit may look upon in hope. As one of those modern heroines puts it: 'Jesus forsaken has filled every void, illuminated every darkness, acompanied every solitude, annulled every suffering, cancelled every sin.'[76] Thinking of

---

73. Text quoted in H. Blaumeiser, *op. cit.*, 403.
74. Olivier Clément, *On Human Being*, London 2000, 14; see Henri de Lubac, *Catholicism*, chapter I, 'Dogma': 1-13 shows how these are the categories of the Fathers, whether Latin, Greek or Syriac.
75. St Peter Chrysologus, *Sermo* 108 in Breviary, Easter, week IV, Tuesday.
76. Chiara Lubich, *Meditations*, London Dublin 1989; see *Il Grido*, Roma 2000.

John's account of the death, Chiara Lubich focuses on Jesus handing over the Spirit (*paredoken to pneuma*: 19:30) and comments: 'When Jesus forsaken suffered, he took away love from himself and gave it to men and women making them the children of God ... Jesus is made nothingness; he gives his all and this all was not lost but entered the souls of humankind. In this way Jesus is truly Mediator: a Nothing that joins heaven and earth because he had already operated this unity in himself.' The fruit of such a love, greater than which none can be thought, is the fact that 'Jesus, having annihilated himself out of love, to the point of making himself *sin, absolute nothingness, hell*, is re-found as the Holy One, the All, God, Paradise, and with himself he made his brothers and sisters, for whom he suffered and died, saints, All, God, Paradise.'[77]

What is fraternal love, then? Look at Jesus crucified and forsaken. He is the measure and the method of love. When two or more of his followers decide, through his grace, to live with the mind of Jesus Christ for each other (Phil 2:5), this love becomes visible on earth, or rather its reflection. And with it the reality of the Father and the fact that Jesus crucified and forsaken is his eternal Son.

'The Father has loved me'

What is particularly obvious in reading the New Testament is the rapport which Jesus has with God. First of all, he calls this God 'Abba'. Joachim Jeremias has shown that such a title of intimacy is so radical and original as to be able to ground the whole of classical Chalcedonian christology. Jeremias wrote that work in 1960, and his insight has percolated in the dogmatic field ever since.[78] Now those who wish to advance the true meaning of Chalcedon with its language of two natures and person 'start instead with what was the centre of Jesus' life and person, according to the testimony of all the gospels: his personal communication with the Father ... The later development of christological

---

77. Text in Hubertus Blaumeiser, *op. cit.*, 405.
78. Joachim Jeremias, *The Prayers of Jesus*, London 1967.

doctrine can be understood as an interpretation of this centre in Jesus' life and death.'[79] Jesus, in fact, 'exists wholly from the Father and wholly towards him. He is nothing of himself, but is in everything from the Father. He is "owed" existence *per se*. He owes himself in a unique way, with everything he is, to the Father.'[80]

This enables us to raise our eyes towards the Holy of Holies, the very event of God as Trinity, where the co-eternal and co-equal Persons indwell each other in an order of procession. The eternal God can transcend himself by going beyond himself infinitely in an expression that is his very equal. In the process he shows who God is. And in the same process he shows us how God is love by the event of this 'self-transcending'. The Father generates the Son out of love, losing himself as it were in the Son since he gives the Son his whole being or substance, so that the Son is 'consubstantial' with him. In the subsequent conflict with the Arians, St Athanasius provided 'the fundamental little rule that all that is said of the Father also is to be said of the Son except that the Son is Son and not Father.'[81] The Father makes himself 'non-being', as it were, in generating the Son, and in this fashion the Father *is*. This is how 'the Father loves the Son'. The Son, for his part, turns towards the heart of this Father (Jn 1:18), recognising that 'he draws his life from the Father' (Jn 6:58), and out of love loses himself in the Father. He lives in him, and in his way makes himself 'non-being' out of love. For this reason he *is*, he is the Son. The Holy Spirit as the mutual love between the Father and the Son and their bond of unity makes himself 'non-being' out of love so that the Father and the Son can meet perfectly as love.[82] God is therefore Three, and yet he is One Being,

79. Walter Kasper, 'One of the Trinity,' in Walter Kasper, *Theology and Church*, New York 1989, 105.
80. *Ibid*.
81. See Athanasius, *Oratio 3 c. Arianos*, 4; MG 26, 330B and comment by Bernard Lonergan in 'The Origins of Christian Realism' in *A Second Collection*, London 1974, 239-262, here 250.
82. See Joseph Ratzinger, *'Der heilige Geist als Communio'* in *Weggemeinschaft des Glaubens*, Augsburg 2002, 34-52.

because a divine Person both is and is not, but even when he is not, he is, because he is a *nothingness of love*.

In fact, 'God is in himself the free transcending of himself towards the Other (Father and Son in reciprocity), he is the very act of this reciprocal transcending (Holy Spirit).'[83] Now it is this love, consisting as it does of 'being-in-the-other', that is the very life and 'lifestyle' of the eternal Trinity. It grounds the possibility of a project 'outside' of the eternal event of the Trinity in creation, incarnation, redemption and recapitulation. Since a divine Person is 'a nothingness of love' in order to be, the incarnation of 'One of the Trinity', will involve an economy of *kenosis*. Christ as the revelation of the design, plan and mystery hidden from all eternity in the Trinity will love the Father to the point of the *kenosis* and the forsakenness of the Father but precisely to give us access through the Holy Spirit to the life and the bliss of our lasting homeland. The very wonder of the hypostatic union, which brings to the eyes of our minds a new and radiant vision of the beauty-glory of the Holy Trinity so that we are caught up in the love of the Trinity we cannot see,[84] opens up a vision of unity and communion that fascinates and attracts.

'As the Father has loved me'

Jesus reveals by the whole gospel of his person, deeds and words, culminating in the cry of abandonment on the wood of the cross, that he has in fact loved us *as the Father loves him*. What a perspective now opens up for us! The measure of his love is literally an infinite measure, a measure that is without measure. This inevitably leads him to 'the hour' of his delivery, to the *kenosis* and to the forsakenness. Because he is the Son of such a Father whose eternal love he now turns towards us, emulating the 'non-being-out-of-love' of his Father, Jesus enters into a 'non-being-out-of love' in our regard. This will involve him in the *kenosis* of the cross and the forsakenness by the Father. 'The

---

83. Piero Coda, *Il Logos e il nulla*, Roma 2002, 207.
84. See Preface I for Christmas; see Hans Urs von Balthasar's commentary on the Preface in *The Glory of the Lord, I*, Edinburgh 1982, 120-127.

sign of a God who annuls himself by becoming man and dying in the most total abandonment, explains why God accepted … all this: it was in harmony with his nature to show himself as love without measure.'[85] In this way, however, he will become the 'father' of the new creation and the 'first-born' of all creation. (Col 1:15) In the birth-pangs of his cry of forsakenness, the new creation will be born (Rom 8:19-22), and men and women will become 'new creations.'(2 Cor 5:17; Gal 6:15)

In the bosom of the Holy Trinity, the Son is an eternal eucharist of thanksgiving to the Father. 'You, Father, are everything, I am nothing.' His very being is a recitation of this eternal hymn of love to the Father as the Source of his Being. Now when the Son becomes man and lives among us in obedience to the Father, as man he continues that paean of praise. He does so as the New Adam and he does so as head and representative of the whole of humankind.[86] He reverses the rebellion of the First Adam. But now the enfleshed Son looks at us, the lost and death-dominated sons and daughters of his Father, now become his brothers and sisters in an infinite solidarity that is pure grace. He looks at us and says, ineffably, 'You are everything, I am nothing.' What the Son says and promises to us becomes fact and grace in the forsakenness that he chooses on the hilltop of Calvary.

We begin now to see how the crucified Son sets up 'from within' and 'from below' a new and universal relationality. The concrete universal, he is both historically 'particular' and absolutely universal and encompassing. This brings us back to the limpid mysterious words of the Christ who prays on the night before he suffered: 'On that day you will know that I am in my Father, and you (plural!) in me, and I in you … May all be one. As you, Father, are in me and I am in you, may they also be one in us.' (14:20; 17:21) Hilary of Poitiers expresses the point vigorously, albeit in nature categories: 'While Christ is in the Father by the

---

85. Hans Urs von Balthasar, *Solo l'amore è credibile*, Borla 1991, 143.
86. See St Thomas on the idea of the 'Grace of the Head' (*'gratia capitis'*), *Summa*, III, q.8, a.5.

nature of his divinity, we on the contrary are in him through his
bodily birth ... From this we can learn the unity which has been
achieved through the Mediator; for we abide in him and he
abides in the Father, and while abiding in the Father he abides in
us. In this way we attain to unity with the Father. For while
Christ is in the Father naturally according to his birth, we too are
in Christ naturally, since he abides in us naturally.'[87]

The 'as': Key to the Art of Loving

As suggested a number of times already, it is necessary to return
to earlier topics *according as their ambiance and implications are put
in place.* The great little word 'as' is one such topic. In chapter
one where we discussed the unfolding revelation manifest in the
public ministry of Jesus of Nazareth, we focused on a lifestyle
that exhibited what we then called 'the art of loving'. Subsequent
chapters, and particularly the current one, invite us to revisit
this art but at a higher level. Since Jesus manifested his ultimate
'lovescape' (Hopkins) in his forsakenness on the tree of the
Cross,(1 Pet 2:24) it is there that one may now read the elements
in his art of loving. In love what is important is to love. In the
crucified and forsaken Son-made-flesh one may read the elements of the art of loving from a higher viewpoint.

There Jesus loves *all*. He loves without limit the whole of creation damaged by the unlove of sin, especially humankind as its
apex and recapitulation. He reveals that this love made into a
sacrifice that takes our sins away (1 Jn 4:10) is offered to all, like
the sun that shines on the grateful and the ungrateful. (Mt 5:45)
Our vocation consists in doing the same, without making dis-
tinctions among people (Jas 2:1-9), except in favour of those
most in need and most in danger.

In the second place, Jesus forsaken *is the first to love*. (Rom 5:8;
1 Jn 4:19) Without love and unable to love, humankind could not
attract the love of the Creator. By first loving us, God the Holy
Trinity makes the ugly beautiful, the dead alive, the empty full,

---

87. St Hilary of Poitiers, *De trinitate*, VIII, 14 in Breviary, Easter, Week
IV, Wednesday.

and the lost found so that there is joy in heaven. (Lk 15:7, 10) Baptised into this Love, it is the basic calling of Christians to be what they are by being like the love that first loved them. Aim at the primacy of loving the others first.

In the third place, Jesus forsaken loves *in the most concrete fashion possible*. He is the one, the only one, who provides what all human beings need, namely, mercy, grace and the life that conquers death as 'the last of our enemies to be destroyed'. (1 Cor 15:26) In a culture that has slithered towards the spectre of what Walker Percy calls 'the thanatos syndrome',[88] he is life lodged and located where its many opposites seem to rule, as if Dionysius replaces Christ. Christians have the glorious calling to be one with all their brothers and sisters whose faces are part-icular faces of that Face.[89] The 'spiritual' and 'corporal works of mercy' take on a new relevance and a new urgency since they serve the least of his and our sisters and brothers.

In the fourth place, Jesus is crucified and forsaken precisely because he made himself one unconditionally with men and women *as they are*. Who could be more one with men and women than the God who became one of them in the incarn-ation in order to be one with them in the sign and reality of the new and eternal Covenant? (Heb 8:6-13; 1 Cor 11:25) He was even made into sin for them, accepting to be led forth outside the city (Heb 13:13) to die the death of the damned. (Gal 3:13; Deut 21:23) Jesus teaches that to love is to make ourselves one in all things except choosing to sin. When we cry with those who cry and laugh with those who laugh (Rom 12:15), the love of Christ is located in hearts that are broken, in bodies that are dis-eased, in relationships that are frayed, in communities that are riven with unlove, and in social or international relations that are undermined by tension and conflict.

Finally, when two or more live this art of loving towards each other, the New Commandment of Jesus, one of the Trinity becomes flesh in our flesh and bone in our bone. The result will

---

88. Walker Percy, *The Thanatos Syndrome*, New York 1987.
89. See Chiara Lubich, *The Cry*, London 2002.

be twofold: first, that unity for which the Son prayed and suffered the abandonment will come into being wherever any two or three such people live or work; secondly, Jesus himself will live in their midst, 'for where two or three are gathered in (his) name, he will be in their midst.' (Mt 18:20)

CHAPTER FOUR

The New Sociality:
an Economy of Communion

That a thing is true, is no reason that it should be said, but that it should be done; that it should be acted upon; that it should be made our own inwardly.[1]

All revealed truth is practical. In fact, 'those who do not love the truth do not yet know the truth.'[2] Obedience is the test, not profession, and still less feeling. The sin in fact is to hear the word of God and not obey it, to 'believe' but not to 'obey'. (Rom 16:26) Faith is authentic when it becomes an obedience to the word and the will of God. (Jas 1:22; Heb 3:7-19; Ps 95:7-11) Over recent chapters, we have been attempting to implement this principle in drawing out the spirituality of divine revelation in some of its core dimensions as these flow from the very fountainhead of that revelation. The Acts of the Apostles could in fact be read in the light of this principle which runs through the pages of scripture from beginning to end.

The concern of the Acts is not to provide a systematic theology of the church. St Luke opts rather to describe how the church makes her way in history: he wishes to show how the followers of the Way, his favourite description of the members of the post-pentecost community (9:2; 18:25-26; 19:9, 23; 22:4; 24:14, 22), begin to make a new history. If in his gospel he describes the journey of Jesus of Nazareth to Jerusalem and so to the cross and resurrection, in the Acts he describes the expansion of the church from Jerusalem to Rome as to the outer reaches and the heart of the *oikumene*. Salvation history converges on Jerusalem

---

1. John Henry Newman, 'Unreal Words,' in *Parochial and Plain Sermons*, vol V, London 1869, 45.
2. St Gregory the Great, *Homily* 14, 3: Breviary, Fourth Sunday of Easter.

only to expand from there to the heart of the known world, symbolised in Rome. A church of Jews becomes in the process a 'church from Jews and Gentiles.'

In just one sentence Luke summarizes the faith-life *and* daily life of this dynamic church. The original community 'remained faithful to the teaching of the apostles, to the brotherhood (*koinonia*), to the breaking of bread and to the prayers.'(2:42) In this fourfold, one encounters a most succinct account of the 'marks' of the church. The church prays and so is holy. By following the teaching of the apostles, the church is seen to be apostolic. By living brotherhood, the church is one. By his account of the gift of the Holy Spirit, in particular the gift of languages that united the whole world representatively present in Jerusalem for the great feast, Luke cleverly shows the 'catholicity' of the church. The church inaugurated finally in the mission of the Spirit of Love, is the reversal of Babel. In fact, 'what Babel scattered the church gathered; from one language there came many; do not wonder: it was pride that did that. Many languages became one; do not wonder: this is what love does.'[3]

This unity and catholicity, however, led to a very concrete lifestyle, or, better, required a definite form. Two chapters later on in his history, Luke summarises this form in these words, 'The whole group of believers was united heart and soul ... None of their members was ever in want, as all those who owned land or houses would sell them, and bring the money from them, to present it to the apostles; it was then distributed to any members who might be in need.' (4:32, 34-35) The church of the apostles solved the social problem overnight. In doing so it revealed the ontological sense of things and their relations to persons. Even more, this church showed the true meaning of being a person: we are when we are *for* and *with one another* unconditionally, in fact, according to the measure of him who first loved us. (1 Jn 4:19; Eph 5:1; Rev 1:5) However, what is even more significant is that the inspiration for this 'communion of

_____

3. St Augustine as quoted by Chiara Lubich, *Tutti siano uno*, Rome 1968, 76.

goods' is strictly revelational in that it flows from the new life communicated by the risen Christ in the teaching of the apostles and in the eucharistic breaking of bread. A new life inspired by the Holy Spirit and leading the community into the mystery of the crucified and risen Christ is in fact the transplanting down to earth of the life of the Eternal Three. In making the generous gift of themselves, the first Christians found their true selves.[4]

St Luke's theology of the church, then, is dynamic, apostolic and liturgical. It inspires the Fathers of the church to see the church as the mystery of the ingathering of humankind into the living Body of Christ. The Christian mystery, in fact, is a mystery of unity. 'For the Fathers, the mystery of Christ is as such a mystery of unity ... This unity is not one theme among others, but the *leitmotiv* of the whole mystery.' This stands out in the fact 'that sin appears as a mystery of separation,' while the mystery of Christ that overcomes sin 'is understood as a mystery of re-unification.'[5] When Henri de Lubac published his epoch-making book *Catholicism* in 1938, he was convinced that 'everything is social in Catholicism' and that this gives rise to 'a parallel development of the interior life and the social life, combining the two in such a way that there is a continual action and reaction between them.'[6] If one accepts, as did the multitude of those who on Pentecost morning heard the first apostolic preaching from the lips of Peter, one enters via Word, conversion and sacrament into the communion of the Body of Christ. Communion is not an option now: it is rather an imperative as the logical consequence of participation in the mystery of Christ. It is only by mutual love as the very law of the new organism of the Body of Christ that the church can live and radiate the light of the glory of God shining on the face of a risen Christ. (2 Cor 4:6) This was the contention of our chapters on mutual love and the measure of that mutual love.

---

4. See *Gaudium et Spes*, 24.

5. Joseph Ratzinger, *Die Einheit der Nationen*, Salzburg 1971, 31, 32; see St Augustine, *Enarrationes in Psalmos* 95,15: PL 37, 1236; St Gregory of Nyssa, *De Hominis Opificio*, ch 15: PG 44, 185 B-D.

6. Henri de Lubac, *At the Service of the Church*, San Francisco 1993, 27.

Nor can such communion or unity be understood in an exclusively 'spiritual' manner. The great originality of Christianity
in fact consists in the unity-in-distinction of God and man in
Christ as well as the consequent unity of the spiritual and the
material, the personal and the communitarian. The Spirit has
been given to the flesh, since the Word has become flesh. 'To
have communion in and with the Body of Christ means to have
communion with one another. It involves acceptance of all others, mutual giving and taking, and the readiness to share one's
goods with others. It is simply incompatible with membership
of the church that some should abound and the others starve.'[7] A
new and dynamic sociality has appeared on earth. It is the living
out of this truth that will manifest the truth of Christ. (Jn 13:35;
17:21) This was the conviction of the Second Vatican Council:
the church's first 'sign' is that of being the living community
since the church is both the sign and the instrument of the unity
of humankind with God and of humankind in itself.[8]

Perhaps just for then?
What emerges with particular vigour in this scheme of things is
the preciousness of the person. Each and every person is a distinct 'You' before his Creator, is addressed by the Redeemer,
and is an athlete indwelt by the Holy Spirit and so in training for
future blessedness, either actually or potentially. 'The affirmation of the dignity and value of the individual person, of his or
her uniqueness and rights, is certainly one of the great inherit-
ances of the West, and in particular, of Christianity.'[9] The concrete implications of such a vision are both radical and inspiring.
'Since every person is made in the image of God, who is one and
three, all people have this model of the Creator within them, expressed in the instinct to enter into a relationship with others.'[10]

7. Joseph Ratzinger, *Weggemeinschaft des Glaubens*, Augsburg 2002, 61.
8. *Lumen Gentium*, 1; 4.
9. Luigino Bruni, 'Towards an Economic Rationality "capable of
Communion"' in Luigino Bruni (ed), *The Economy of Communion*, New
York 2002, 42.
10. Chiara Lubich, 'The Experience of the "Economy of Communion"'
in Bruni, *ibid.*, 14.

This dignity stood out with particular clarity in the Trinitarian revelation of mutual love among infinite Persons, each of whom lives wholly for and in the Others. Since this living-in-the-other means a dying-to-oneself, a trinitarian alterity comes into view, albeit dimly. 'The fullness of each person coincides with the "self-emptying" entailed in being *wholly for* the other.'[11] Each divine Person both *is* and *is not*, but even when he is not he is, since he is a *nothingness of love*.

Alas! something tragic has happened in the course of Western history: the person made for relationship declined into the 'individual' increasingly presumed to be self-sufficient. In fact, as has often been noted in these pages, the definition of the person that gained the ascendancy, during the middle ages and over all others, was that of Boethius: 'The person is an individual substance of rational nature.' The person is an individual, sufficient in and for himself. The implications of this for the subsequent development of the West are now plainly evident. They belong, however, to another investigation that is quite outside the scope of this work. Suffice it to say here that the notion of the person as individual facilitated the reduction of the Divine Sociality of the Divine Trinity to a way of individual redemption. The second commandment had been absorbed into the first. The substance of revelation sustained major loss in consequence, the injury to the church on her journey through space and time was incalculable, and the proclamation of the gospel to the whole of creation slowed down. The point is reinforced when one remembers that 'being one mind and one heart' was now seen as clearly optional, attributable to a miraculous beginning of the church but relevant only for monasteries and religious communities ever since that privileged age of the church's foundation.

An Alternative Economic Vision
As of September 2001, almost eight hundred businesses spread

---

11. David Schindler, 'Towards a new Unity of the Disciplines' in *The Abba School*, New York 2002, 8.

out over the globe declared themselves to be the advocates of an 'economy of communion'. All of these belong to an 'ecclesial movement' called the Focolare Movement or, to give it its official title from the Catholic Church, *The Work of Mary*. This movement began under the bombs that dropped unceasingly on the city of Trent during the final two years of the Second World War. Chiara Lubich and her young friends made the discovery of mutual love as the pearl of the gospel and lived this out in the context of the mutual hatred that drove the cruel all-consumptive conflict raging around them. Inspired by a 'spirituality of communion,' Chiara's followers set out on a personal and collective adventure. While visiting in 1991 her numerous friends in Brazil who had been living this gospel-inspired spirituality of unity, Chiara Lubich launched the project of an 'economy of communion'.

Over 246 of the businesses in the adventure are located in Italy, a further 172 are situated in Western Europe, 191 are in South America, while a significant number are in North America, Asia and Australia. These businesses operate according to a logic of solidarity. Thus profit is distributed in three parts: the first is reinvested in the business, the second goes to help those in need, and the third is used to develop educational structures for the formation of men and women motivated by a 'culture of giving'. Without 'new people' it is not possible to generate a 'new economics' for a spring cannot rise higher than its source. And it is certainly not possible to develop a new economics that is the genuine measure of the human person. The movement has inspired even more businesses since 2001 and has modified the way in which many existing businesses are run.[12]

To understand the phenomenon of the economy of communion – many doctoral dissertations have already been written on the subject at universities around the world – it is necessary to

12. For some general literature in English on the Focolare Movement, see Edwin Robertson, *Chiara*, Belfast 1978; *Catching Fire. The Spiritual Ideal of the Focolare Movement*, Guildford 1993; Jim Gallagher, *Chiara Lubich. A Woman's Work*, New York 1997; www.focolare.org

go back some decades in time, in fact to the last years of the
Second World War when efficient hostility destroyed brutally
both life and property, either killing or dashing the hopes of millions. In the town of Trent, at the foothills of the Dolomites and
near the entrance to the Brenner Pass, a young woman, Chiara
Lubich, had, together with her companions, made a great discovery: they had discovered God to be love. This led them to believe in love (1 Jn 4:19) and to live coherently with that conviction. (Jn 14:23) Under a particular grace, as becomes obvious
with hindsight, they had decided to make God the ideal of their
young lives. Providence led them to take up the gospels; they
took them with them when they had to run to the air-raid shel-
ters which was a frequent daily occurrence. They read those divine
Words which seemed strangely practical, albeit challenging, and
decided to put them into practice at once.

The Holy Spirit illumined in a particular way for the members of this movement the words about charity as if to highlight
the principle: 'A man who does not love the brother that he can
see cannot love God, whom he has never seen.' (1 Jn 4:20) They
translated these words into practice in the most concrete fashion
and made a discovery that fascinated them: the words in the
gospels were meant to be lived *and* they 'work'! In situations of
dire poverty and hopelessness in war-torn Trent, they would
visit the sick, the aged and the wounded offering them whatever
clothing, food, jam, firewood and medicine they had. As they
did so, the amount of goods donated to them – food, clothes,
basic medicine – increased enormously. 'This pattern of distrib-
ution and help continued throughout the war … as Providence,
a visible sign of God's blessing on the work being done.'[13] The
experience was an ongoing discovery of the Father who counts
the very hairs on our heads. 'Give, and there will be gifts for
you: a full measure, pressed down, shaken together, and running over, will be poured into your lap.' (Lk 6:38) The heavens

---

13. Lorna Gold, *The Sharing Economy*, Aldershot, England and
Burlington VT, USA, 2004, 70.

opened and they knew that they were not orphans any longer but beloved daughters of the same Father. (Jn 14:18)

By attempting to live the words of the gospel they discovered that we are all God's children and therefore are members of one family, regardless of colour, creed, nationality, sex or age. 'The world vision of this movement is centred on the reality of God who is the Father of all. It follows that if God is Father, then all people are called to live as sons and daughters of God and, hence, as brothers and sisters in universal brotherhood, the fore-taste of a more united world.'[14] The gospel, in fact, is the Father's blueprint as to how to live life in that family. As such, it is the very alphabet of Christians: only by learning to translate it into daily life could they achieve the literacy appropriate to the children of God. Not only that, but if one tried the adventure of living those 'words of life,' (Phil 3:13) the world around began to change. Most of all, however, the world within, the real world in their young hearts, changed.

Chiara Lubich and her companions had no intention whatsoever of starting a 'movement'. On the contrary, they wished only to live, to live for the Father and for his Son whom the gospel taught them to recognise in the face of each brother and sister, particularly in those who suffer. It was he whom they wished to serve with concrete deeds of love. (Mt 25:30-45) By the end of the war in 1945 there were over 500 people in the town of Trent and its environs who were living by the gospel of unity expressed through mutual love for each other and in the practical assistance offered to an increasingly numerous needy. 'By 1949 there were just over 3000 members of the Focolare mainly in the north of Italy. Since then, the Focolare has expanded both geographically and in terms of the kinds of involvement. Focolare records count around four million adherents, with a quarter living in Latin America and another quarter in Western Europe.'[15] The DNA of the vast Movement – there are members in over 192 countries – was determined literally under the daily bombard-

14. Chiara Lubich, *ibid.*, 14.
15. Lorna Gold, *ibid.*, 50.

ments of the city of Trent. That DNA highlighted Jesus' prayer for unity (Jn 17:21f), his new commandment of reciprocal love (Jn 13:34; 15:12), and his cry of abandonment on Calvary as both the authentic measure and stamp of that love – the forsaken Jesus lost everything for his Father except love for his Father and for us. (Mk 15:34; Mt 27:46) And from that gospel insight there flowed out into the church and into humankind a pure river of life and light, which was simultaneously and indivisibly a spirituality and, as time has told, a divine-human sociality.

Towards a Gospel Culture

As the Focolare spirituality of unity spread through the whole church, into the other Christian churches and communities, into the great religions – there is a thriving dialogue with the Buddhist, Hindu, Jewish and Muslim faiths – and also among men and women of other convictions, a new culture began to spread silently in many nations. Within the Focolare Movement this 'culture of giving' has been distinctive from the very beginning. From the gospel-inspired deeds of concrete love in war-devastated Trent between 1943 and 1945 this culture became the very lifestyle of an enlarging movement of people. Thus the members assisted, by means of a 'communion of goods', the thousands of fellow-members throughout the world who lived below the poverty line. In that way, these needy brothers and sisters could live a life worthy of their true dignity. The Movement was being prepared by God for the launch, in Brazil in May 1991, of the actual 'Economy of Communion'.

Why did that new development occur in fact in Brazil? The 250,000 poor people still in the Movement in Brazil made everyone realise that the communion of goods was no longer enough. 'It was then that the idea came to increase the communion of goods through giving rise to businesses, which would be entrusted to competent people who would be able to run them efficiently so as to make a profit.'[16] The businesses represent a broad range of economic sectors from pharmaceutics through

16. Chiara Lubich, *ibid.*, 15.

banking and manufacturing to financial services. They are in harmony with the numerous individual and collective efforts of those who try to 'humanise' the economy. Perhaps it was the originality of the Economy of Communion and its openness to like-minded economic efforts that inspired the holding of a day-long seminar on the theme at the Smurfit School of Business in UCD in February 2004.

Now it is obvious that such a view and practice in economics is diametrically different from the economic policies pursued by large agencies and global economic institutions. 'Within these organisations, the dominant economic practices and ways of understanding the goals and objectives of economic action are going in exactly the opposite direction. They privilege the radical affirmation of the individual as an agent, leading to policies dominated by unfettered consumption that have disastrous consequences not only for human communities but for the environment and ecosystem too.'[17] This logic reinforces a certain view of human beings according to which the human being is a producer and consumer. One is made for the economy, the economy is not made for one.

How did this state of affairs come about? And in the Christian West? As this study has repeatedly stressed, revelation shows the human person to be essentially a relational being: one's capacity for loving communion with God and with one's fellows in the mystery of the Blessed Trinity is what distinguishes human beings. This capacity also ennobles them just as its abolition pains them. Made in the image and the likeness of God the Holy Trinity, they become what they are in the measure in which they live by relations expressive of the capacity to love. However, what emerged in the West, from the time of humanism,[18] was rather the idea of the 'autonomous individual.'

To add to the paradox, it was the Christian culture that largely

---

17. Vera Araujo, 'Personal and Societal Prerequisites of the Economy of Communion' in Luigino Bruni (ed), *ibid.*, 22.
18. See Eugenio Garin, *L'umanesimo italiano*, Bari 1947.

gave rise to capitalism, as Max Weber shows.[19] Revelation showed up creation in the most positive light, and asked the person to 'subdue the earth.' (Gen 1:28) Fledgling economic science began to stress, particularly in the nineteenth century, the total autonomy of the individual in the pursuit of wealth. 'The premise that set in motion Western science, and also economic science, was this: there are no inseparable bonds linking the various aspects of reality ... But economists did not only distinguish and separate out the sphere of the "search for wealth" from the others: they also brought about another separation ... Economics starts from the premise that individuals are not linked to each other by inseparable bonds before beginning to barter. The intellectual exercise of separating the *ego* from the *alter* is, therefore, possible, giving rise to an individualistic science in which "I," as an individual agent, can be analysed independently of my relationship with the other.'[20] The profit motive becomes central, the individual has no duties to others, and wealth brings no responsibilities for the rich. The maximisation of personal advantage became the goal and the motivation of the economic enterprise. *Homo economicus* had been born.

Towards a We-Rationality

The phrase has begun to be used recently by some authors. Two English thinkers, one a philosopher and the other an economist, have begun to reflect on the concept of a 'we-rationality'. In his *Trust within Reason*, Martin Hollis sets himself the task of rethinking the very nature of economic rationality in such a way that it can find a sense of sociality while remaining within the realm of reason. His point is that 'Trust makes sense, given a different concept of rationality.'[21] Such a concept 'does not destroy sociality, but strengthens it.'[22] Hollis is typical of a group of

19. See Max Weber, *The Protestant Ethic and the Spirit of Capitalism*, Los Angeles 1991; Robert Sirico, 'The Economics of the Late Scholastics', *Markets and Morality*, February 1998, 122-129.
20. Bruni, *ibid.*, 44.
21. Martin Hollis, *Trust within Reason*, Cambridge 1998, 161.
22. Bruni, *ibid.*, 52.

philosophical economists who see that the reduction of reason to
the exclusive service of individual advantage and economic gain
is a very limited use of reason, and, in what concerns us here, is a
very limited expression of economic rationality. In this expression, 'reason guides us in satisfying our desires in the best ways,
but does not question the content of the desires themselves. This
means that behaviour will be judged not on the basis of its intrinsic content, but rather on its capacity to obtain those results.
It is easy to see how such a vision of rationality provided an easy
way for values and intrinsic motivations of actions to be omitted
from economic science.'[23] This perspective is so vigorous that it
swallows up all interpersonal relationships within its logic.
Even friendship, in spite of its noble Aristotelian definition, is
only an instrument of this kind of reason: friends are good because they are useful.

The second author is Robert Sugden who in his *Thinking as a
Team* tries to explain the authentic rationality that is operative in
the collective view and practice of economics. A person motivated
by a we-rationality 'values his actions as part of a whole made
up of the actions of all the team members: for that reason an
action is rational inasmuch as it is part of the actions as a whole,
which, taken together, have produced good results.'[24] This
seems to be a collective individualism, if one may so speak, since
it remains within the paradigm of means and ends. In an authentic we-rationality, however, the priority lies with belonging,
with duty, with love, in short with the overall interpersonality of
persons. For it to function, 'there is a need for a kind of person
who could be called *homo donator*, who is capable of giving rise
to the category of gift or sharing within public activities and, in
particular, within economic ones.'[25]

*Anthropological and Theological Prerequisites of the Economy of
Communion*
The economy of communion clearly presupposes a definite view

23. *Ibid.*, 46-47.
24. Richard Sugden, *Thinking as a Team*, 1993, 86.
25. Vera Araujo, *ibid.*, 22.

of reality. It expresses a way of seeing, judging and acting that stresses certain first principles. Among these are the imprint of the blessed Trinity as the revealed core of all reality, the primacy of persons, a culture of giving, a yearning for solidarity or communion, and a particular understanding of rationality.

The economy of communion is based on a sense of unity that has specific presuppositions. These are rooted in the main in the mystery of the triune God who is love. The study of this mystery engaged us at some length in the chapters on the blessed Trinity and on the Law of the Trinity. There we saw the centrality of the mystery after its long banishment into the regions of seeming irrelevance. There has been a recovery of its inspiring centrality for life and action in our times. The economy of communion is a shining instance of the mystery since it 'applies' the mystery in a most visible fashion, becoming a *vestigium trinitatis* in the process. It perceives the Trinitarian love where each divine Person lives in and for the Others, and then seeks to mirror that love by expressing it in a concrete economics that is made for man. The result is 'an economy on a human scale,'[26] an economy according to the revealed measure of man. In the words of Chiara Lubich, 'the actors within the Economy of Communion businesses seek to live out, in the particular way that their productive organisation requires, the same lifestyle that they live in the other areas of life.'[27] As 'new persons' (2 Cor 5:18; Gal 6:15) attempting to live out concretely the event of eternal mutual love that is the Holy Trinity, they apply a Trinitarian logic to the running of their businesses. These businesses, in fact, could only exist and develop *on the foundation of this new humanity that is the net outcome of the mystery of Christ and the Holy Spirit* in the church.

The economy of communion, secondly, is something new because it comes from persons who are new. They are new because they aspire to 'have the mind of Christ' (1 Cor 2:16) and so they attempt to live and direct their businesses according to the mind

---

26. Bruni, *ibid.*, 12.
27. Chiara Lubich, *ibid.*, 18.

of Christ. (Phil 2:5) In that way they turn the 'new we' that Christ has brought on earth, a we that participates in the eternal We of the Blessed Trinity, into a concrete dynamic that drives their businesses. The people in the economy of communion reach after that 'something extra' by which they open up to others and are liberated from exclusive preoccupation with themselves and the pursuit of profit as the only good. Only new people can generate a new economics, for economics will always embody the particular treasure inhabiting people's hearts. For the new men, women and children who love the dying wish of Christ that all be one (Jn 17:21), the treasure is that their work and entrepreneurship build unity among as many children as possible of the one Father. Faith becomes fact, hope inspires daring projects, and love made flesh in the most varied businesses begets a new *homo oeconomicus*.

The economy of communion inspires, in the third instance, a culture of giving, for it is vigorously committed to a primacy of giving over having. In that way it goes against the current of much of contemporary economic practice and theory, challenging what Pope John Paul calls 'the civilisation of "consumption" or "consumerism," which involves so much "throwing away" and "waste".'[28] It does not even begin with giving of *things*, but rather with the giving of *oneself* because it is grounded in the conviction that we are each created as a gift for the others, 'as the Father in the Trinity is everything for the Son, and the Son is everything for the Father.'[29] As already stressed, persons see themselves as a gift for the others, while the others become gifts. All this happens in the theatre of a freely chosen reciprocity. 'The culture of giving encapsulates both the essence of the person ... and a whole series of attitudes and behaviours that characterise human relationships ... In other words, the culture of

28. Pope John Paul II, Encyclical Letter *Sollicitudo Rei Socialis*, 28; see *Gaudium et spes*, 24.
29. Chiara Lubich, *Writings*, September 2, 1949 in Judith Povilus, *United in his Name: Jesus in our midst in the Experience and Thought of Chiara Lubich*, New York 1981, 67.

giving is about the nature of the human person as a being who is open to communion, to a relationship with the Absolute-God, with the others and with creation.'[30]

Of course, not every kind of giving results in the culture of giving. Too often perhaps 'the very act of giving underscores the inequality between us. Charity, alms, doles-out do not establish neighbourliness, friendship or equality. Indeed, they often make things worse, especially if they are impulsive, patronising, ill-considered.'[31] There is a giving that seeks a certain control over the others. This is a subtle form of domination. There is, secondly, a giving that seeks pleasure and satisfaction in the giving: it trumpets forth for all the fact that one is a giver. (Mt 6:2) The recipients of this counterfeit giving see themselves as the pawns in the pseudo-giver's vanity and self-display. Then there is a kind of utilitarian giving which, in the famous phrase, gives in order that the recipient would give back something. There is, however, the giving that is truly according to divine revelation. This is the giving that Jesus praises. 'You received without charge, give without charge.' (Mt 10:8) 'There is more happiness in giving than in receiving.' (Acts 20:35)

Within the Focolare-inspired view of giving, 'the role of the person who is in need is accorded a very high position. Since possessions are given secondary importance, the value of the person is judged not on their capacity to have or give materially but on their capacity to give themselves to others ... Need is not regarded as something inherently negative, of which to be ashamed, but rather a situation which can enable sharing to be put into practice among the community.'[32] Such a perception flows directly from the Word of God and so it is both a gift and a task. It opens up vistas ordinarily hidden from human consciousness but then asks us to translate these same vistas into daily reality. In Christianity, in fact, every good idea is a responsibility.

30. V. Araujo, *ibid.*, 23.
31. Duncan B. Forrester, *On Human Worth: A Christian Vindication of Equality*, London 2001, 3.
32. L. Gold, *ibid.*, 78.

In the fourth place, there is the rediscovery in our times of the core spirituality of Christianity, namely, the 'spirituality of communion'. In his illuminating Letter for the third Millennium, *Novo Millennio Ineunte*, Pope John Paul II wrote words that are inspirational if the life of the church is to correspond to the designs of God's heart and not disappoint the deeper expectations of the men and women of our times. He says, 'To make the church *the home and the school of communion*: that is the great challenge facing us in the millennium which is now beginning, if we wish to be faithful to God's plan and respond to the world's deepest yearnings.' (43) This can remain an abstraction, a vaporous aspiration, unless Christians translate this divine-human imperative into, among others, concrete economic action. As the same Pope already affirmed in the encyclical *Sollicitudo Rei Socialis*, 'Beyond human and natural bonds, already so close and strong, there is discerned in the light of faith a new model of the unity of the human race, which must ultimately inspire our solidarity. This supreme model of unity, which is a reflection of the intimate life of God, one God in three Persons, is what we Christians mean by the word "communion".'[33]

Finally, this communion is also a sociological and economic category, or rather can inspire such categories. In that way, it points towards a fresh economic rationality which enjoys both revealed and rational legitimation, being truer to God and to man. The fact is borne out very concretely and attractively by the economy of communion. For as we have seen, this adventure arose out of the spirituality of unity discovered by Chiara Lubich and her companions. Since in the logic of God, the few are the benefactors of the many,[34] the gift made to the few has now become the inspiration of an expanding multitude around the world. The economy of communion, in fact, is a practical embodiment of gospel inspiration. The Russian sociologist, George Gurvitch, for example, sees communion as a sociological and economic category. Communion is 'the manifestation of real

---

33. Pope John Paul II, *Sollicitudo Rei Socialis*, 40.
34. A favourite formula with John Henry Newman.

sociality.' 'Reciprocal immanence between [the] self, the others and us finds its apex in communion,' while 'those who participate in communion feel like they are lifted up by a liberating breeze which eliminates all obstacles, freed from themselves and all the social ties which could be a hindrance to them.'[35] Of course, Gurvitch is not here thinking of the Christian concept of communion in itself since he is not looking to the revealed eternal model of such communion. Still, his insight points both to the originality of the revealed model and its capacity to enter into dialogue with all valid efforts to put the human person at the root of all reflection on the structuring of society on every level – social, systematic, structural and institutional.

To sum up the economy of communion, it is necessary to make the clear distinction between gratuity and reciprocity. The philanthropist gives to others but he does not seek any rapport with them. The volunteer, however, inevitably generates relationship with those among whom he works. The volunteer labours not only *for* the others, but also *with* them. That labour generates inevitably 'relational goods'.[36] In that fashion, the volunteer is clearly different from the philanthropist. The ancient Roman writer, Seneca, in his tenth letter to Lucilio, puts the point poignantly: 'Human madness has reached the point where doing big favours for someone has become very dangerous: he, in fact, because he regards it as shameful not to return his exchange, would like to remove his creditor. There is no greater hatred than that which is born from the shame of having betrayed a creditor.'[37] What the Roman philosopher dimly perceived was powerfully addressed by the eternal Wisdom who became flesh, lived on earth and prayed that 'all may be one as [the Father] and I are one' (Jn 17:21). In the economy of communion, the bedrock is mutual love, the pearl of the gospel. This

---

35. George Gurvitch, *La vocazione attuale della sociologia*, Bologna 1965, 165, 207.
36. Stefano Zamagni, 'On the Foundation and Meaning of the "Economy of Communion" Experience,' in Bruni (ed), *The Economy of Communion*, 130-140.
37. *Ibid.*, 131.

mutual love, in the measure of Jesus' loving us to the point of the abandonment, pre-empts the very idea of a 'rich us' and a 'poor them', since, as we have just seen, the other is always the brother/sister without whom there cannot be reciprocity and unity.

What has happened through the spirituality of unity, as lived by the Focolare Movement and as applied in the field of economics, could also occur in other fields of human endeavour. A good example might be the field of politics. The truth is that it has in fact already begun to emerge there: the *Movimento per l'unità* has recently appeared and the result is a burgeoning unity-in-distinction between parties across a broad political spectrum.[38] Otherness is then the presupposition of unity, and unity is the crowning of otherness. In that way a 'new politics' comes into view. This politics is at the service of the whole polity since it preoccupies itself with the common good of the polity.

All this shows that the life that Christian faith discovers is in fact an inspiration for the building of the earthly city. That earthly city ought to bear the image of the City of God, for it cannot be sufficient of itself but must rather point its citizens towards the city that is to come. (Heb 13:14) To put it the other way around, divine revelation seeks translation into daily life, specifically into those fields that constitute the forces that shape human society and determine the future agenda of the human family. In the final analysis this is the reason for the highly dramatic character of church history: do her children live by the gospel of unity? Only persons born from the 'total newness brought by Christ' (Irenaeus) can generate a new economics or a new politics or a new art in the earthly city. In other words, dogma without spirituality is barren – a skeleton without the flesh, but spirituality without dogma is enthusiasm or even Gnosticism – the flesh without the skeleton.

---

38. See Enzo Maria Fondi, Michele Zanzucchi, *Un popolo nato dal Vangelo. Chiara Lubich e i focolari*, Milano 2003, 523-529.

CHAPTER FIVE

Towards a Trinitarian Ontology

The mystery of life flows all around us. In that stream we understand ourselves in a matter-of-fact manner initially.[1] Only with
the passing of time and the opportunity it affords for reflection
do we raise the questions that lead to explicit insights. Only with
time do we discover the values of which our lives are *already* the
expression. A reflective lifestyle, however, begins generally
within a set of particular experiences. Sometimes one dramatic
encounter with the mystery of sorrow or joy is enough. Very
often this encounter is of the former kind, or we may assess it as
being such at the time. However, it awakens us to ask the essential questions, if not formally and verbally, at least personally
and existentially. As one contemporary philosopher puts it,
'True philosophy begins when one "wakes up" at a certain moment of life and discovers that one exists ... One enters
into philosophy by means of this "awakening" which is experienced in being and by existing. This means that philosophy is
born when one becomes vividly aware of existing and of being
challenged to provide a clear and limpid response to all the
problems that present themselves ... What characterises philosophical thinking, then, is not the discursive or reasoning element, but the profound perception of what is real by means of
the discovery of one's own existence.'[2] The door to philosophy
and reflective existence, then, passes through each person's
heart: it has to open there for the good reason that it cannot open
anywhere else.

1. See Hans Georg Gadamer, *Wahrheit und Methode*, Freiburg-im-
Breisgau 1965, 261.
2. Pasquale Foresi, *Conversazioni di filosofia*, Roma 2001, 12, 13 (translation my own); see Stanislaw Grygiel, *Extra Communionem Personarum
nulla Philosophia*, Roma 2002, 52.

An illuminating instance of this awakening is to be seen in the case of Fyodor Dostoyevsky (1821-1881). His experience is very apposite in our particular context. As a young man of twenty-eight years, Dostoyevsky was sentenced to death. He was led before the firing squad expecting certain death. Those terrifying last minutes focused his mind on the stark facts of life and death, justice and cruelty, hope and despair, which are in any case abiding facts of human existence. The execution protocol, however, was only a mock one. Instead, the sentence was commuted, and he was sent into penal servitude in Siberia, 'the house of the dead'. There 'he was humbled into naked Christianity'.[3] That close encounter with the mystery of death caused a great change of mind in him. The transformation that came over him, however, was much more than an appreciation of getting a second chance, as it were, to live the one and only life he had. It was something far greater: it was the discovery that 'an idea stronger than any calamity'[4] is necessary if human life is to have *unconditional* meaning. This 'idea' Dostoievsky found realised in the mystery of Christ, especially in the mystery of the crucified Christ. This discovery is the immediate inspiration of 'the three novels with a universal vision: *The Idiot*, *The Brothers Karamazov*, and *The Devils*.'[5]

To awaken to the fact *that I am* is therefore a wonderful development. It is a first necessary step on the road to self-realisation. This awakening, however, leads to a second: the world does not need me in order to be. I am not necessary to the existence of the world that surrounds me. This comes home to me very powerfully when I see that I am only one among many other persons. It is reinforced further the moment I realise that my own hold on life, on existence, is weak, even vulnerable. I exist, but my existence is not necessary to the world: the world is able to exist quite well without me. Here I encounter the paradox that, though I

---

3. Hans Urs von Balthasar, *The Glory of the Lord*, volume V, *The Realm of Metaphysics in the Modern Age*, Edinburgh 1991, 189.
4. Fyodor Dostoievsky, *Raskolnikov's Diary*, ed Fuelop-Miller (1928), 417.
5. Von Balthasar, *ibid.*, 189-190.

exist, my existence is not necessary. I make the experience of 'non-being', and realise the 'penury' of my own hold on being. 'If it is true that philosophy arises from the "awakening" to the perception of being, it could also be said that it arises from the affirmation of not being. The truth is that that surprise at existing which is at the origin of philosophy implies the wonder of noticing that one should not have to exist ... In other words, we notice that we exist but that we are not being.'[6] I have existence, indeed, but I am not existence.

This shakes the foundations of my life, indeed, but that very shaking makes me search for the House of Being that is strongly built. (Ps 122) It turns me, in the measure in which the wonder at my being and non-being is activated, towards Another who is. I may even ask the question, why is there something and not simply nothing? In that way the question first formulated by Leibniz in the eighteenth century and influentially recovered by Martin Heidegger in the last, returns. It does so in spite of the 'weak reason' that Newman diagnosed already in the 1830s, as we have seen in chapter two, and which has been operative ever since, particularly in the realm of those more lasting questions that will only cease to be asked when the sun ceases to shine, the earth ceases to rotate and the winds cease to blow.

The Situation of Ontology Today

Still, our age is not interested in ontology which is *the science of being and existence*. In the light of the 'humanness' of philosophy, its closeness to both our humanity and the human condition, this is a paradox to say the least. Whereas a cow when left alone begins to chew the cud, a person left alone may begin to ask serious questions. The science, or rather metascience, of ontology is of interest only when questions concerning being and existence are both present, articulated and pursued.

Our times are marked by unheard of progress in the realms of science, industry and technology. The outflow of goods from this development acts as a kind of distraction from the abiding

6. Pasquale Foresi, *ibid.*, 15.

questions to which we have just alluded. These goods affect the human condition profoundly, engendering a consciousness that forgets an earlier wonder, the wonder that anything *is*, that we *are* and that things *exist*. In spite of the fact that Leibniz raised the unavoidable question, why is there something and not simply nothing, as early as the eighteenth century, Heidegger could complain, in the last century, that 'Being had been forgotten'. Modern men and women are much more interested in *what things are* – and surely there are wonderful and seemingly endless numbers of them – than in the fact that *they are* in the first place. Essence has eclipsed being. The how-questions have crowded out the why-questions. In such a milieu, ontology is irrelevant and forgotten. Still, the great mystery of our humanity remains, and is all the more mystifying perhaps for the very fact of its trivialisation.

The result is that the question that the human being *is* can never quite disappear. It can indeed be glossed over or relegated to the pre-scientific or 'the older philosophy', according as more fashionable notions control the market square or the academy, what Alexander Solzhenitsyn called the prejudices and the idols of any age.[7] But in the measure in which it will be forgotten or banished, the depth of our humanity will be correspondingly diminished because unrecognised and so unrealised. Blindness to the being of things leads inevitably to blindness to the God of all beings. T. S. Eliot seems to capture the mood of our age as it affects the prospects of ontology and religion when he looks at the idols of the marketplace of his day,

> These are usual pastimes and features of the press,
> And always will be so when there is distress of nations
> On the Edgeware Road or on the Asian shore.
> Men's curiosity searches past and future
> And clings to that dimension. But to apprehend
> The point of intersection of the timeless
> With time, is an occupation for the saint –

7. Alexander Solzhenitsyn, *Cancer Ward*, London 1968, 460-477; see Joseph Ratzinger, *Principles*, 52f.

No occupation either, but something given
And taken, in a lifetime's death in love,
Ardour and selflessness and self-surrender.[8]

The Impact on Theology
Now this state of affairs has had its impact on theology. Many
currents of theology in fact show an aversion to ontology. An al-
leged 'Hellenisation of dogma' is invoked: Greece has destroyed
Israel. The philosophy of concept and substance from Greece
has subverted the Semitic culture of image and event. This
stands out, continues the contention, in the metaphysical and
unbiblical language in which the dogmas of christology and
Trinity were formulated.[9] Since the central truths of faith have
been hijacked in this fashion, the faith has become quite 'unbiblical'. Thus some contemporary theology prefers a history of salvation approach. It locates the events of biblical saving history
within the panorama of other religions. The result will largely be
a comparing and contrasting of Christianity with other religions. The faith, hope and love that result from revelation and
that seek understanding will move to another planet and another
time. In that milieu faculties of theology will tend to become institutes of religious studies.

A second approach attempts to bypass the need for ontology
by an anthropological reduction of the mystery of faith.[10] Here
theology states what is unique to revelation by relating revelation to the enduring human problems. Imperceptibly revelation
suffers reduction: theology no longer attempts to say what
revelation contains, what revelation wants to show, to give and
to say to humankind. It measures the unfathomable riches of
Christ by the questions we can formulate. It forgets that Christ is
not only the answer to all questions, but actually questions all

---

8. T. S. Eliot, *Dry Salvages*, V.
9. See Bernard Lonergan, 'The Origins of Christian Realism' in *A Second
Collection*, London 1974, 239-262.
10. See Hans Urs von Balthasar, *Love Alone the Way of Revelation*, London
1968, chapter II: 25-42.

answers that can be given now or in the future. He will always be the Ever More.

A third approach lifts God beyond his own revelation. He is the hidden and unknowable mystery. As the *Deus absconditus*, he is beyond even his own self-revelation. The great dogmas about Christ and the Trinity must then disappear in a great cloud of unknowing. They attempt to say what cannot be said, and end up pretending to say too much. This state of affairs could have been prevented if the God of creation and the God of the 'new creation' had been kept in touch within the one universe of being or reality.

Theology and Philosophy: the Historical Legacy

It is a fact of history that the gospel quickly entered into dialogue with philosophy. We have had occasion to reflect on this in chapter two dealing with faith and reason. The case of Justin Martyr is perhaps paradigmatic: 'I have found this (the gospel) to be the only true philosophy.' The philosophies existing around the Mediterranean enter into the early elaboration of 'the word of faith'. (Rom 10:8) In that way the church initiates during the early centuries a dialogue with Neo-Platonism, Stoicism and, to a lesser extent, with the thought of Aristotle.

In this context it is instructive to look, however briefly, at the actual encounter of revelation and philosophy in the third century. The instances of Tertullian (160-240) and Origen (254) may be taken as typical. Tertullian found very happy formulae for expressing Christian doctrines – in fact, we owe to him the first coining of the terms eventually employed in the doctrine of Christ and Trinity. However, there are formulae in his christology that shock. He could write: 'There was a time when there was not sin to make God a judge nor a Son to make God a Father.'[11] Underlying the theology of Tertullian is the ontology that all reality is corporeal, including the soul and the angels, though each having its own particular mode of corporeality. What is incorporeal is non-existent.[12]

11. Tertullian, *Adversus Hermogenes*, 31.
12. Tertullian, *De Carne Christi*, 11; *De Resurrectione Carnis*, 11, 53; *De Anima*, 7.

As for Origen of Alexandria, he stressed the strict immateriality of both the Father and the Son. At once we see that 'the basic contrast lies in differing notions of reality. For Tertullian the real had to be bodily; it was ... the already-out-there-now of extroverted animal consciousness. But for Origen the real was ideal, as in middle Platonism.'[13] Since the Father and the Son are distinct, they had to be the reality of distinct ideas. The Father was goodness itself, but the Son was good only by participation.[14] Origen is under the control of his ontology: the real is the ideal. It is this that determines much of his theology, just as Tertullian's opposite ontology determined much of his theology. These two giants of the early church are two specimens who show the impact of existing ontology on the work of theological reflection on the data of faith.

A Convergence of Indicators

I am, but I am not being. My hold on being, on life, is fragile. The tension that results makes me search for that which *is* simply and unconditionally. In the final analysis is human existence meaningful? Or is it ultimately without meaning? The seriousness of these concerns is heightened when one looks at some paradigmatic moments of human life and existence. To some of these paradigmatic experiences we now turn. They will put flesh and blood, as it were, on the abiding questions. We will select three experiences where the answer to these questions is stronger than mere hints and guesses.

a. The 'Thou-I' Relationship of Mother and Child

Philosophers, psychiatrists and theologians are all drawn to the study of that most primordial of all human relationships, namely, the relationship between child and mother. In this first experience, which is already operative while the child is still in the womb, the child experiences, primordially and pre-conceptually,

---

13. Bernard Lonergan, 'The Origins of Christian Realism' in *A Second Collection*, London 1974, 239-262, here 248-9.
14. Origen, *De Principiis*, 1, 2, 13.

a Thou who is unique. Since the mother loves the child unconditionally, the child is progressively and profoundly affected. This
makes the beginning of the child's existence in the world a journey into wonder. The child feels let into being. Not only, but to
exist for the child is to be loved. This unconditional love of the
mother radiates the light of being over the most vulnerable
stages of the child's existence.

The child knows that the mother loves him/her unconditionally. The being of the child is 'held' within the being of the mother,
in the womb indeed, but also after birth and during the vital first
months and years. To be for the child is not to be from himself
and of himself, but to be from and of the mother. The child perceives, preconceptually, that existence consists in being loved.
To be is to be loved immensely. *Diligor, ergo sum*: I am loved,
therefore I am.

There results an important further perception on the part of
the child: being is not only love, being is also beauty, goodness,
truth and unity. Such love in fact is beautiful, it diffuses goodness, it shows truth and it builds unity. The child's first encounter with existence is therefore an encounter with 'the very
colours of reality,' (Hemmerle) with what the tradition calls the
'transcendentals of being'. The child holds his existence from
another, and that other is love. To be is to be irradiated by the
beauty, goodness and truth of this love. This stands out in the
fact that the first deployment of speech by the child is never self-
directed, but mother-directed, for the first word is always,
'Mammy'. It is never the word 'I'. I can say 'I' only when a 'You'
has first loved me.

The mother, however, enables her child to make this experience of life and being because she has first loved that child. Her
love is not sentiment: it is very concretely the gift of herself. Her
love consists in loving. She shows that what matters in love is to
love. By living for her child she enables that child to be, to love to
be, and to rejoice in the good of being and in the beauty of being.
The 'new substantive' is the verb, the transitive verb. Her concrete loving 'transubstantiates' her own substance into her child

in the first instance, but also transubstantiates the substance of her child. She is not (she does not live for herself) so that the child can be. She is a nothingness of love and out of love, for her loving says in effect to the child: 'You are everything, I am nothing.' In her we can read the truth that 'a person is an entity of a type to which the only proper way to relate is love.'[15] Aquinas saw this when he wrote, '*Amor est nomen personae.*'[16]

b. The 'Great Mystery': Marriage (Eph 5:32)
In the scriptures of the First and Second Testaments, human marriage is a central reality. God's covenant with humanity illuminates the meaning of marriage. Marriage in its turn illuminates God's unfolding covenant-relationship with humankind. This mutually illuminating relationship completes the hermeneutical circle. 'In sending his Word among us, God chooses to "need" a partner, who will be in a relationship of communion with him and through whom his Word can communicate his Trinitarian life to the world. This is the reason for Paul's wonder at "the great mystery" of Christ and the church (Eph 5:32).'[17]

The human, historical and theological depth of marriage, then, invites us to consider marriage as an indicator both of the human mystery and the meaning of reality. For marriage involves the encounter of man and woman in a bond that not only throws light on the relationship of God to humankind and history, but also on the mystery of God the Holy Trinity. A phenomenological look at the unity of man and woman in marriage will serve to continue our investigation of being and reality.

This becomes more obvious the moment one remembers the further revelation that occurs in the opening of Genesis providing the foundational principle of anthropology. That principle states that man and woman together are made in the image and likeness of God. (Gen 1:26-27) If we knew and understood better

---

15. John McNerney, *Footbridge towards the Other*, London New York 2003, 158.
16. St Thomas, *Summa*, I, q.37, 1 c.
17. Breandán Leahy, *The Marian Profile*, New York 2000, 52.

their mutual gift, then we would understand better the being of God of whom they are the very image.

The words from the Yahwist account of the creation of man and woman provide our entry point. 'This is why a man leaves his father and mother and joins himself to his wife, and they become one body.' (Gen 2:24; Mt 19:5; Mk 10:8) The 'exodus' from one's family of origin culminates in the formation of a new family. That exodus presupposes the love that expresses itself in self-giving. St Augustine's principle that 'they begin to depart who begin to love ... For their walk of departure is a movement of the heart,'[18] comes into view: it encapsulates the insight and suggests its applicability. Man is willing to give himself to her, woman is willing to give herself to him. Love here is the love that consists in giving, in fact in the making of oneself into a gift to and for the other. And this happens mutually. This mutuality introduces a new principle into the I-Thou relationship, namely, the mutual being-for-each-other. 'In the "unity of the two", man and woman are called from the beginning not only to exist "side by side" or "together", but they are also called *to exist mutually "one for the other"*.'[19]

To be authentically human, then, requires each one to aim at making the sincere gift of self. In fact, 'to say that man is created in the image and the likeness of God means that man is called to exist "for" others, to become a gift.'[20] Such a mutual gift between man and woman makes them 'one flesh.' They constitute a unique communion. They are a 'We', and this communion is something more than any I-Thou relationship. In fact, 'the We-Communion is that form of the human plural in which the Person most fully realises himself as a subject.'[21] Rudolf Allers

---

18. St Augustine, *Enarrationes in Psalmos*, Psalm 64, 2.42-44, as translated by Eric Voegelin in *Published Essays 1966-1985*, Baton Rouge 1990, 105.
19. John Paul II, Apostolic Letter *Mulieris Dignitatem*, 7: the italics are in the original.
20. *Ibid.*
21. Karol Kardinal Wojtyla, '*Person: Subjekt und Gemeinschaft*' in K. Kardinal Wojtyla, A. Szostek, T. Styczen, (eds), *Der Streit um den Menschen*, Kevelaer 1979, 13-68, here 54.

saw this clearly many decades ago when he claimed that 'fellow-human love is the objective medium of human existence.'[22]

When the individual acts on his own initiative, his action expresses his being, and he is the efficient cause of that action. However, when the individual acts in concert with others, who are other selves, there is a greater realisation of the I. The something more at the heart of the We-Communion of man and woman points in the direction of a further depth. This is the depth that appears in the fruit that issues from that We-Communion, the child. The child is the sign and the proof that authentic love has to bear fruit. In losing themselves *for* one another they find themselves *in* another, a third person. The child signals the depth dimension of mutual love between man and woman. This line of thinking also raises the exciting question of what interpersonality might imply and generate when lived out among the many.[23]

This very brief look at the mystery of man and woman reinforces the insight gained in our study of the mother-child relationship for our understanding of reality. To be is to love, to love is to give, and to give is to give oneself totally. This involves non-being, indeed, but it is the non-being of love on the part of the mother, in the first paradigm of mother and child, and on the part of both husband and wife in the case of marriage. However, it is a non-being that is not the negation of being. Rather, as deep love it is the fullness of being. Just as when one gives a gift one loses something (non-being), but thereby becomes something more through generosity and thoughtfulness (more being), so too in each of these paradigms 'a law of being' comes into view, namely, 'I am when I am not *out of love.*'

This 'law of being' through the non-being of self-giving begins to throw a radiant light over the whole of reality. 'The

22. As quoted by Werner Löser in 'Being interpreted as Love: Reflections on the Theology of Hans Urs von Balthasar', *Communio*, XVI: 4 (1989), 481. Hans Eibl reads Plotinus as tending in the same direction, *ibid.*
23. See Thomas Norris, 'Why marriage is one of the seven Sacraments' in *The Irish Theological Quarterly*, LI, 1 (1985), 37-51.

human being becomes a person not primarily through what he himself does. Rather he is already given to himself with an inalienable dignity and an inalienable level of being. Nonetheless, the person's level of being and dignity consists precisely in the ability to transcend and to realise himself, and this in relationship to another. Now communion and the "We" go beyond the mutual relationship of an "I" to a "Thou".'[24] Those who live in this fashion will the more readily understand this analysis of the chosen paradigms and their associated phenomena, while those who do not live in this fashion may not see or perceive. Not everyone hears music, not because there is no music, but one may be deaf; not everyone sees the beauty of nature, not because there is no beauty, but because their eyes do not see.

c. The Other as Neighbour

In a conference on the future of Europe, the famous philosopher, Hans-Georg Gadamer, underlined the importance of the 'other' in these words: 'We have to learn to stop before the other as other ... we have to understand the other and others as the other of ourselves, in order to participate one with the other.'[25] The enlarging literature on the 'Other'[26] is indicative of the discovery of forgotten truths concerning the human person. At the risk of oversimplifying, one could say that a particular metaphysical notion of the human being had taken over. This notion was largely founded on the famous definition which Boethius had given of the human person in the eighth century, namely, 'the individual substance of rational nature.'[27] This definition followed the metaphysical tradition, and had the merit of identifying the individuality of the human being. In doing so it also identified the irreducibility of the person.

24. Klaus Hemmerle, *Wegmarken der Einheit*, Munich 1995, 246.
25. H.-G. Gadamer as quoted by J. McNerney, *op. cit.*, 34 from Gennaro Cicchese, *I Percorsi dell'altro: Antropologia e Storia*, Rome 1999, 21.
26. The names of Buber, Marcel, Ebner, Scheler, Rosenzweig, Mounier, Levinas, and Wojtyla stand out in a particular way. See Bernhard Caspar, *Das dialogische Denken*, Freiburg-im-Breisgau 1967.
27. Boethius, *Liber de persona et duabus naturis*, 3: PL 64, 1343; see St Thomas, *Summa*, I, q. 29, a. 1.

However, this definition had a huge demerit: it left out the relational dimension and sunk the personal into substance. Although Aristotle saw quite clearly that 'a friend is another self (*alter ipse*),'[28] this had not extended itself into the deployment which Christians had made of the great Stagirite. It is perhaps no exaggeration to say that the philosophical movement of phenomenology in the last century was the result of the reaction to this 'cosmological reduction' of the human person.[29] The human being is not just a particular 'specimen' of the species *homo sapiens*, rather he is a personal subject. Neither is he to be locked into what Robert Sokolowski calls the 'egocentric predicament' by which his thought and experience are within a bubble or else contained in a Cartesian cabinet.[30] Not only, but he is understood best in that relational dimension: his actions serve to manifest his subjectivity that becomes itself in the encounter with the subjectivity of the other. This 'relational portrait of the person'[31] shows the 'other' as another 'I' in the same humanity. He or she is not 'other *than* me' but 'the other *of* me'. The point is well expressed by Gandhi: 'I cannot do harm to you without doing harm to myself, because I am part of you.'[32]

In order to be a person, it is necessary to recognise the equal dignity of the other. S/he and I are equal expressions of one and the same human nature. The other is thus a reminder to me of my own dignity. This is so powerfully true, in fact, that in a Levinasian sense, 'the various philosophies of nihilism, personalism, deconstructionism, and of otherness can be seen as clearing the site for an adequate philosophy of the human person.' It is the contention of Levinas that 'modern antihumanism which

---

28. Aristotle, *Magna Moralia II*: see James McEvoy, 'The other as oneself: friendship and love in the thought of St Thomas Aquinas' in James McEvoy and Michael Dunne eds, *Thomas Aquinas. Approaches to Truth*, Dublin 2002, 16-37.

29. See Robert Sokolowski, *Introduction to Phenomenology*, Cambridge 2000.

30 Ibid., 9.

31. John McNerney, Footbridge towards the Other, 79.

32. Mahatma Gandhi, in Wilhelm Muehs, *Parole del Cuore*, Milano 1996, 82.

denies the primacy that the human person [has for itself] ...
clears the place for subjectivity positing itself in abnegation, in
sacrifice, in a substitution which precedes the will.'[33]

The unspeakable phenomenon of Auschwitz has evoked two
conflicting responses. For Theodor Adorno, Auschwitz as the
greatest pulverisation in history of the human person raises the
question unavoidably as to whether philosophy and poetry will
ever again be possible. 'In the concentration camps it was no
longer an individual who died, but a specimen.'[34] Interestingly,
it was two inmates of the same man-made hell who provide responses at the other end of the spectrum. They are Viktor Frankl
and Maximilian Kolbe. Famous is the discovery by the former of
'the meaning of his slow dying': in the vivid recollection of his
wife's love, he discovered not only the existential 'other' as another I in the same humanity, but also as the symbol of the ultimate meaning of his existence. 'For the first time in my life I saw
the truth as it is set into song by so many poets, proclaimed as
the final wisdom by so many thinkers. The truth – that love is
the ultimate and highest goal to which man can aspire. Then I
grasped the meaning of the greatest secret that human poetry
and human thought and belief have to impart: *The salvation of
man is through love and in love.*'[35]

The case of Kolbe is well known. The very Nazi record of his
substitution for an unknown other prisoner has the golden
gospel words, which are surely quoted unintentionally: 'On the
14th August 1941 he gave his life for another prisoner.' (Jn 15:13)
When Pope John Paul visited Auschwitz in June 1979, he indicated the purpose of the camp as that of 'trampling underfoot
radically, not only love, but all the signs of human dignity, of
humanity.'[36] Kolbe's deed, however, shows both the meaning of
being a person, a fulfilled 'I', and the true dignity of the other as

---

33. Emmanuel Levinas, *Otherwise than Being*, Pittsburgh 1999, 127-8:
quoted in McNerney, 35.
34. Brian O'Connor (ed), *The Adorno Reader*, Oxford 2000, 88.
35. Viktor Frankl, *Man's Search for Meaning*, London 1987, 36.
36. Pope John Paul II, 'Omelia del 7 giugno a Oswiecim-Brezezinska,' in
CSEO *Documentazione*, 305.

another 'I' of equal dignity precisely because an 'I' of the same humanity. In *Crossing the Threshold of Hope,* the pope writes these words: 'The person is a being for whom the only suitable dimension is love ... Love of a person excludes the possibility of treating him as an object of pleasure ... it requires the affirmation of the person as a person.'[37]

What opens up in this perspective is 'the basic dyadic ontological structure of all being, that is, presence in itself and presence to others.' To this can be added a third primordial relation which consists in receptivity and which is also constitutive of being, and is what is lacking in a particular way in all contemporary reflection on reality. The result of this is that 'we should describe every created being as possessing its own existence from another, in itself, and towards others – a triadic rather than just dyadic structure.'[38] Secondly, in the husband-wife paradigm, the orientation towards others is highlighted: to be is to love, and to love is to give, to give truly is to give oneself completely. The ethos of reality as communion comes into view. To be is to live for the other with the measure of being willing to die for the other.

This becomes obvious the moment one looks back at the particular paradigms of experience we have been considering. In the mother-child paradigm, one could observe the relation of receptivity. The child receives his existence *from* parents, a fact underlined by the linguistic priority of the mother: 'Mammy' precedes universally the 'I' of the child. To be is to be loved and so to be from. The ethos of reality as gift implying receptivity is in the forefront. Next, in the paradigm of the 'other,' we saw that the I reaches true self-determination, self-governance and self-possession, in a word, true being, only when the I recognises the 'other' as *another* 'I', and not as *other than* 'I.' Since this is not a

---

37. *Idem, Crossing the Threshold of Hope,* London 1994, 200-1.
38. W. Norris Clarke, *Explorations in Metaphysics: Being – God – Person,* Notre Dame, Ind, 1994, 119. The relevance of this to the understanding of Mary in the whole economy is obvious and exciting. See further David L. Schindler in dialogue with Norris Clarke in *Communio,* 20 (Fall 1993), 580-620.

merely speculative truth but one laden with practical import, the 'I' sets out to live by the principle that the other is to be loved. Substance and relation are in harmony. To be is to be *for* and to love the other in the truth of our shared humanity and personhood. Finally, in the husband-wife paradigm, the mutuality of persons, their free but necessary interpersonality, is highlighted: to be is to love one another, to love one another is to give to one another, and to give truly to one another is to give oneself to one another. The ethos of reality as communion comes into view. To be is to live *for one another*.

These phenomenological descriptions of three primordial human paradigms may be only the 'emergency rations' of interpersonal relations, and the last source of warmth in an era of cold.[39] Still, even these poor, albeit undeniable, manifestations of love begin to X-ray human existence. They show up our human being as it were.[40] They do so in spite of the fact of an advancing blindness to the light of Being. This blindness may make them look less probable. Still, the fact that men and women are in the image and the likeness of God will mean that any authentic insight we have thereby gained into our human being through these 'indicators of love' should now throw light on the prototype. That prototype has revealed himself as a Trinity, 'three Persons equal in majesty, undivided in splendour, yet one Lord, one God.'[41] Now Trinity is not an abstract theory imposed on the history of revelation, but the only possible explanation of the originating experience of divine revelation.[42] Trinity in truth is the very shape and form of God's dealings with the human family which then opens up to the human family their access to, and participation in, the very rhythm of Trinitarian life.

39. Hans Urs von Balthasar, *The Glory of the Lord*, VI, 649.
40. See Olivier Clément, *On Human Being*, London, New York, Manila 2000 for a fascinating treatment of this theme drawing from the riches of the Greek Fathers and prominent contemporary philosophers.
41. Preface for the Trinity.
42. See John Thompson, 'Barth and Balthasar: An Ecumenical Dialogue' in Bede McGregor OP, and Thomas Norris, eds, *The Beauty of Christ*, Edinburgh 1994, 171-192, especially 182-186.

Perhaps a certain similarity will now stand out enabling us to understand a little the great mystery of the most Blessed Three-in-One. Is this the case? Joseph Ratzinger has this to say: 'The real God is by his very nature being-for (Father), being-from (Son), and being-with (Spirit). Man, for his part, is God's image precisely insofar as the "from", "with" and "for" constitute the fundamental anthropological pattern.'[43] Of course, our goal is an understanding of reality, an ontology of Being. Hopefully what we have just done has pointed us towards such an understanding. Perhaps it has suggested a certain heuristic of the desired ontology. Maybe this ontology will even include the dimensions of love and person, relation and mutuality, self-gift and self-emptying? Must it not also include what have been called the transcendentals of Being – beauty, goodness, truth and unity?

Trinitarian Ontology: the Access
It is the facts of divine revelation, however, that indicate the best route of access to a genuinely Christian ontology. As we have seen in chapter four on Israel and Christ, God gradually accommodates himself to the human condition until, in the fullness of time, there occurs the fullness of revelation. St Irenaeus formulates that principle so poignantly: 'The Spirit came down on the Son of God, who became the Son of man, and with him became accustomed to dwell in the human race and to abide in God's creation, within men, working the Father's will among them and making their old natures new with the newness of Christ.'[44] The God of Jesus Christ so accustomed himself to our human nature and human condition that he actually aimed at the cross from the moment of the incarnation. The cross and the Trinity are the two great mysteries of the faith, with the cross revealing the mystery of the Trinity and how the Blessed Three involve themselves in the drama there played out. This mutual indwelling –

---

43. Joseph Ratzinger, 'Truth and Freedom' in *Communio* XXIII: 1 (1996), 28.
44. St Irenaeus, *Against the Heresies*, III, 17, 1.

perichoresis is the word employed by the later Greek Fathers[45] –
of Trinity and cross identifies the genuine access to our understanding of reality, being. This ontology has to be a Trinitarian
ontology.

Perhaps we can now formulate the principle of access to this
ontology. 'If God reveals himself to humankind, if God speaks
to humankind a divine Word, all that must happen in a human
word.'[46] When God speaks his Word he has to speak it in ca-
dences intelligible to the addressees. In the language of Irenaeus,
God 'accustoms' himself radically to humankind. The converse
of this is also true, namely, human words, particularly the
'word' of humanity and history become capable of being employed by this God to 'say' the divine. In order to do so, however,
they must 'transcend' themselves towards 'the invisible things
of God.' (Rom 1: 20) God hands over his Word so radically into a
human word that what is uniquely his, the divine, is only attainable in the human Word. The point is made with matchless clarity in the First Preface for Christmas: '… through the mystery of
the incarnate Word the new light of your brightness has shone
onto the eyes of our mind; that knowing God visibly, we might
be snatched up by this into the love of invisible things.'[47] It is the
principle so succinctly enunciated by St Augustine: 'Through
humanity to divinity.' The sacred humanity of the Son is not
only the instrument of the eternal Word, it is more accurately the
expression of the Son. How could we perceive the divine Son if
not in the humanity which he took? Here we encounter the
'christological analogy of Being' which is perhaps the real context for understanding properly the metaphysical analogy of
Being.

---

45. St John Damascene, *De fide orthodoxa*, I, 14; see Gisbert Greshake,
'Perichorese' in *Lexikon für Theologie und Kirche*, 8, Freiburg-im-Breisgau
1999, 31-33.
46. Klaus Hemmerle, *Thesen zu einer trinitarischen Ontologie*, Einsiedeln
1985, 14.
47. This translation is found in Hans Urs von Balthasar, *The Glory of the
Lord*, I, Edinburgh 1982, 120.

Trinitarian Ontology: the Historical Deficit

The Christian revelation, then, has impacted human thought profoundly. It has indeed been influenced by the culture of Greece and Rome into which it was first inculturated. It has providentially borrowed from that culture the linguistic and philosophical tools it needed. Some speak of a certain Hellenisation of dogma. However, the very history of the first ecumenical councils repeats the message that the church did not let the culture dominate or appropriate the revelation. Referring to the early christological councils, Walter Kasper writes: 'Any kind of divine-human mixture or intermediary is inconceivable on Christian grounds. Thus Chalcedon, just as Nicaea, says in Hellenistic terms something that is quite un-Hellenistic, in fact, anti-Hellenistic.'[48] The early councils did not surrender the originality of the gospel to the categories of Hellenism. Some language it had to use to communicate to its environment. Another language it did not have as soon as it left the realm of Jewish culture to begin its mission to the nations.

Still, it is true to say that 'what is specifically Christian did not ultimately refashion, in an original and lasting way, the anticipatory understanding of the sense of being and the presentation of ontology.'[49] In this lies the bimillennial drama of Christianity, the roots of her cultural crisis in recent times, as well as the challenges posed today. True, there have been great fragments of such formulation. It is enough to think of St Augustine toiling over the multi-volume *De trinitate*, of an Aquinas employing Aristotle's categories to work out a comprehensive *theoria* of processions, Persons, and relations in the Trinity, as well as his insistence that '*esse* is what is most intimate to every being and most profound in all things.'[50] It is touching to stand before the Francis-inspired theology of Bonaventure with its threefold of emanation, exemplarity and

---

48. Walter Kasper, '*Einer aus der Trinität*' in *Theologie und Kirche*, Mainz 1987, 217-227; see also his *The God of Jesus Christ*, New York 1984, 233-63.
49. Klaus Hemmerle, *Thesen*, 22.
50. St Thomas, *Summa*, I, q.8, a.1; see I, q.4, a.1 ad 3.

reduction. One could continue to mention the fragments worked
out by the geniuses who adorn the arches of the church's history,
like great constellations in the heavens.

What is distinctively Christian sheds its light over the whole
of reality. This light illuminates reality, the mystery of Being.
Since the mysteries of the Trinity and the paschal mystery of the
cross and the resurrection and sending of the Holy Spirit constitute the core of divine revelation, it is their light that must
illuminate our understanding of being. Our ontology, in a word,
has to be a Trinitarian-Paschal ontology. Christ is the key to the
mystery not only of finite being but also to 'the mystery of the
Source of being, the transcendent communion of love which we
call the Trinity.'[51] This means that 'Being and love are co-exten-
sive.'[52]

The how? question immediately asserts itself. Hemmerle answers in terms of a 'differential analysis'. This analysis can be
stated as the question: What difference does faith in Jesus Christ
make to our understanding of God, humankind and the world
when this faith breaks in upon this understanding?[53] If God becomes man so that men and women can become God by participation – the principle the Fathers loved to reiterate – what does
this fact tell us about human being, the being of the world, the
being of history? This question has the indispensable merit of
holding in tension the reciprocal *a priori* of philosophy and theology, namely, that human word and being is capable of expressing the divine, while the divine will accommodate to the human.
'Since God is Trinity, and this Trinity has appeared in our history,
then the fundamental human situation, our thinking and our
being, experience a reversal. This reversal overtakes the canon
of all "pre-existing" human thought about God, the self, the
world and Being.'[54]

51. Aidan Nichols OP, *Mysterium Paschale*, Edinburgh 1990, 5.
52. Hans Urs von Balthasar, *'Der Zugang zur Wirklichkeit Gottes,'* in
Mysterium Salutis, vol II, Einsiedeln 1967, 17; quoted in his 'Being interpreted as Love' in *Communio*, XVI: Fall 1989, 475-6.
53. See Second Vatican Council, *Optatam Totius*, Decree on the
Formation of Priests, 15.
54. Klaus Hemmerle, *Thesen*, 18.

Both St Augustine and St Bonaventure introduced a phenomenology of love into their speculation on being. They did so as a result of their perception that love is the ontological core of all the mysteries of faith. Famously, St Augustine formulated the principle: 'If you see charity, you see the Trinity. For you see the one who loves, the one loved, and the love that unites them. And you see only three.'[55] As he wrote the fifteenth and concluding book of the great work, he looked back with nostalgia and regret: he saw that this phenomenology of love and loving was in fact the moment when his understanding of the mystery was both most profound and most accessible to us limited and sinful creatures. We have addressed this issue in chapter nine on the Trinity where we saw that, in the light of such phenomenology, Augustine discovered and employed the category of relationship to expound his Trinitarian theology. This fact was not only a tremendous breakthrough in relation to the fruitful grasp of the great mystery itself, it was also a breakthrough in our understanding of reality.

Many contemporary authors have stressed the novelty that emerges here in our understanding of being.[56] The ultimate and highest reality is not substance but relation. 'The meaning of being is to be found in self-communicating love.'[57] Following Augustine, St Thomas arrived at the definition of a divine Person as 'subsisting relation'.[58] Now it is one thing to work out this insight in theology: it is quite another to transpose it into anthropology. In the event Thomas did not shed its light on the mystery of the created person nor apply it to the society of created persons. True, he did employ Aristotle's understanding of friend-

---

55. St Augustine, *De trinitate*, VIII, 8, 12.
56. See Anthony Kelly, *The Trinity of Love*, Wilmington 1989, 185; Walter Kasper, *The God of Jesus Christ*, London 1984, 154-156; Joseph Ratzinger, *Introduction to Christianity*, San Francisco 1990, 135-6; 'Concerning the Notion of Person in Theology' in *Communio*, XVII: Fall 1990, 439-454; John Zizioulas, *Being as Communion*, New York 1985. For an overview see Patricia A. Fox, *God as Communion*, Collegeville 2001.
57. Walter Kasper, *ibid.*, 156.
58. St Thomas, *Summa*, I, q. 29, a. 4.

ship to an analysis of charity among Christians.[59] But it is significant that Aristotle's category of relation does not feature strongly there.

The question governing the elaboration of ontology was, what remains and what passes? Substance remains, the accidents pass. This is the answer of Aristotle. However, the answer of the New Testament to the question is remarkably different: it is love that remains. (1 Cor 13:12) The Lord of History has told us that the meaning of history is in loving, so that we already know the questions that will be put at the last judgement. (Mt 25:30-45) Still, our metaphysics depends rather on the insight of the great Greek. It has not thought itself through in the light of the revelation of love as the core to the mystery of being, both created and uncreated. 'If what lasts is love, then the centre of gravity shifts from the self to the other, and both movement (not in the Aristotelian sense) and relationship (*relatio* no longer understood as a category, as the most insignificant accident of being) go to the centre of the stage … Only one thing remains, participation in that movement which love (*agape*) itself is. This movement is the very rhythm of being. It is the rhythm of that rhythm that gives itself.'[60] This insight, or rather this revealed perspective, 'would surely have resulted in the expansion of philosophy's world-bound ontology.'[61] It gains its truth from the way God has lovingly dealt with his creation. It can only be true, in other words, 'if a Wholly Other, who is himself love, allows his love to become so effective in the world that all values will thereby undergo a transvaluation.'[62] The entry of such a love has happened as a matter of fact and of history. Furthermore, it has happened within the setting of the *a priori* reciprocity of theology and philosophy.

---

59. *Summa*, II-II, q 25.
60. Klaus Hemmerle, *Thesen*, 38.
61. Hans Urs von Balthasar, *Theo-Drama, V, The Last Act*, San Francisco 1998, 73.
62. Werner Löser, 'Being interpreted as Love,' *Communio*, XVI: Fall 1989, 482-3.

Setting out from what is distinctively Christian

The two core mysteries of Christian faith are the Trinity and the cross. The two are intimately correlated with the result that one accesses the Trinity via the mystery of the cross, since 'the self-giving of Jesus is the self-giving of God himself ... Everything is inserted into the rhythm of the origin's self-giving.'[63] It is on the cross that one discovers what the Trinitarian *agape* is, as the First Letter of John stresses. (4:8, 16) It is there that we learn the logic of the life of the eternal Persons in their absolute unity. On the cross one learns the length and the breadth, the height and the depth of the love of the Blessed Three shining on the face of the enfleshed Son (2 Cor 4:6; Eph 3:19) who locates this very love 'economically' for us men and for our salvation. There we receive all the love of the Father of our Lord Jesus Christ. There the Son speaks out both his and our 'Yes' to the Father even to the point of experiencing 'god-forsakenness'. It is on the cross that the Word is fully unfolded in our humanity and our human condition, telling us all that which he wants to tell of the Father and manifesting to the Father all that which he wishes to communicate to him about us. The cross is the place where he commends his Spirit into the hands of the Father (Lk 23:46), but donates him to us (Jn 19:30) 'If one wishes to speak of unity and the Trinitarian life, the cross is the nodal centre; it is only there where he has taken every single individual within himself, not leaving anything outside his suffering and the transformation of that suffering into pure love, that there can be unity.'[64]

The cross, it has to follow, is that place where all our why's are gathered, linked together and then sent soaring upwards in the Son's great Why? Here one encounters a logic of loving which, because it is a loving done by the divine Persons 'for us' – to use the recurring pre-Pauline phrase (Mk 10:45; Mt 26:28; Lk 22:19-20; John 6:51; 1 Cor 15:3-5) – is quite literally an 'onto-logic of Loving'. Here one notices a 'trinitarian ontology', not as a speculative truth about God, but as the discernible pattern of

---

63. Klaus Hemmerle, *Thesen*, 27.
64. *Idem, Partire dall'unità*, 109.

something lived 'to the end' (Jn 13:1) and in perfect historical fulfilment (Jn 19:29) of the purpose hidden from all eternity in God. (Eph 1:9) Here one becomes capable of 'perceiving' (Eph 1:18), with 'the eyes of the heart', the internal logic of that Love which is God himself. Now one sees why St John explains that his short formula of faith, 'God is love,' must always be connected to those summit-events of salvation history, the giving by the Father of his Son to be the sacrifice offered for our sins. (1 Jn 4:9)[65] And here one gains an insight into 'the free necessity' (St Anselm) of the repeated New Testament formula: 'It was necessary that the Christ should suffer and so enter into his glory.' (Lk 24:26)

We begin to glimpse something of the eternal mystery of God as a Trinity of Persons each of whom loves the Other Persons infinitely. In the words of Chiara Lubich: 'The Father generates the Son out of love, he loses himself in the Son, he lives in him; in a certain sense he makes himself "non-being" out of love, and for this very reason, he *is*, he is the Father. The Son, as echo of the Father, out of love turns to him, he loses himself in the Father, he lives in him, and in a certain sense he makes himself "non-being" out of love; and for this very reason, he *is*, he is the Son. The Holy Spirit, since he is the mutual love between the Father and the Son, their bond of unity, in a certain sense he also makes himself "non-being" out of love, and for this very reason, he *is*, he is the Holy Spirit.'[66] The very summit of Being is love, the life of loving among the Persons.

Each divine Person both is and is not. But even when he is not, he is because he is a 'nothingness of love'. In this way the Persons 'incorporate' 'non-being' among them, the 'non-being' of loving which consists in 'being-the-other'. Not only is the Father not the Son, but the Father exists for and in the Son. As for the Son, he exists for and in the Father, not in himself. As for

---

65. See the comment of Hans Urs von Balthasar, *Die Wahrheit ist Symphonisch*, Einsiedeln 1972, 56.
66. Chiara Lubich, 'Towards a Theology and Philosophy of Unity' in *An Introduction to the Abba School*, introduction by David L. Schindler, New York 2002, 24.

the Holy Spirit, he exists not in himself but in the Father and the Son, enabling their encounter and making that encounter 'fruitful' in both creation and the New Creation. And it is precisely this 'non-being' through loving that makes possible, in the ministry of the second Person on earth, the 'non-being' of the cross. The 'second *kenosis*' (Phil 2:8) on the cross is the clash between the 'non-being' of the Son's self-giving to us, and the 'non-being' of our 'No's' to this self-giving throughout our history. Here two expressions of 'non-being' encounter, that of the 'non-being' of self-giving and that of the 'non-being' that negates Being. The former reveals Being as love, the latter is the denial of Being by the refusal to love.

The cross results from the Son's 'being in us' and 'being for us' to the very end when he takes into himself all the 'No's' of human history to himself and his Father. Thus the mysteries of the cross and the Trinity manifest that Being is the eternal event of loving, and that creation is re-created for one and one only purpose, namely, to participate in this very rhythm of loving that gives its own rhythm to creation. 'Father, may they be one *in* us, *as* you are in me, and I am in you, so that the world will know that you have sent me.' (Jn 17:21) Without a trinitarian ontology it will not be possible to witness to the God of Jesus Christ in our world, the 'new evangelisation' will be undermined from within, and the great areas of human achievement in the arts, science, medicine, communications, politics and technology will remain 'outside' the heart of an increasingly privatised and individualised Christian faith.

The circle of loving can be described in this manner. 'God is love; love is giving oneself; giving oneself means losing and becoming nothing; but being nothing is the expression of the love which is God. In that way, in nothingness and the losing of God there is fullness, and that fullness is once more a giving and a losing of oneself in nothingness. This circle, this permanent Pasch, this being consumed in nothingness and by means of nothingness, in him, is the circle of our life.'[67]

---

67. *Ibid.*, 121.

With his usual perspicacity, Søren Kierkegaard glimpsed this truth of a trinitarian ontology. In *The Journals* one finds this quote: 'We *must* hold fast to the belief that when God – so to speak – decides to write a play, he does not do it simply in order to pass the time, as the pagans thought. No, no: indeed, the utterly serious point here is that loving and being loved is God's passion. It is almost – infinite love – as if he is bound to this passion, almost as if it were a weakness on his part; whereas in fact it is his strength, his almighty love: and in that respect his love is subject to no alteration at all.'[68] The cross, then, is the disclosure-revelation of the very life of God. This life consists in the Trinitarian loving which is the eternal God. That life is love, not as an attribute, but as that eternal dance of being in loving, giving, receiving and uniting.[69] We see, in other words, that 'what is primary is not the substantial noun (substantive) but the transitive verb; we begin "with happening, action, consummation." But "to give oneself" is not to lose oneself; it is the essential realisation of oneself. *Ekstasis* and *enstasis* are one, simply the two sides of the same thing.'[70]

The access, then, to the being of God is in and through the mystery of the crucified and risen Lord. This is quite fascinating, and is so for many reasons. We have just seen some of those reasons. They should perhaps be recalled. There is the pedagogical value in the fact that God should so 'accustom' himself to us: the cross is the icon of the Trinity where the drama of Trinitarian loving has a final dramatic encounter with humankind in the flesh and history of the eternal Son. Then there is the double *a priori* of God and his creation resulting from the wonder of the incarnation. This keeps theology and philosophy in dynamic tension with each other, theology requiring philosophy, and philosophy being challenged to go beyond itself in true self-transcendence. Thirdly, there is the wonderful fact that one

68. Søren Kierkegaard, *The Journals*, quoted as the epigram of Hans Urs von Balthasar's *Theo-Drama*, V, 1998.
69. See C. S. Lewis, 'Beyond Personality: or First steps in the doctrine of the Trinity' in *Mere Christianity*, London 2002, 153-227.
70. Hans Urs von Balthasar, *Theo-Drama*, V, 74.

catches a glimpse of that loving that constitutes the very life of the Trinity. In the fourth place, all of this remains practical: one begins, in other words, to discern an art of loving, and to read in the lives of fulfilled Christians what has been aptly called the 'metaphysics of the saints'.[71]

Still, it could perhaps be objected that this approach glosses over the fact of evil, pain and sin. The plausibility of this objection is more apparent than real. The objection, in fact, only serves to highlight further what has been stated, namely, that our access to the reflexive light of the blessed Trinity on reality occurs precisely in and through the cross of the Son. And there the all-holy Son became sin for us (2 Cor 5:21; Gal 3:13) 'so that in him we might become the goodness of God.' (2 Cor 5:21b) All is integrated here into the all-connecting and all-healing design-mystery of the Trinitarian self-givings. (Rom 8:32; Gal 2:20; Jn 19:30)

Trinitarian Ontology as underpinning the Art of Loving

What remains, then, is love, or rather loving, since, as Chiara Lubich so clearly saw, 'in love what counts is to love'.[72] We have been able to focus on the significance of the revelation that God is love and therefore also trinity. The three divine Persons are relationships of love, and God is one because each Person is 'non-being out of love'. 'In the light of the Trinity, Being reveals itself, if we can say this, as safekeeping in its most inner recesses the non-being of Self-giving: not the non-being that negates Being, but the non-being that reveals Being as love: Being which is the three divine Persons.'[73] It is now time to list and describe the components of such a trinitarian ontology.

I. RELATIONALITY

Our phenomenological paradigms earlier in the chapter had

---

71. *Idem*, *The Glory of the Lord*, V, Edinburgh 1991, 48-140.
72. Chiara Lubich, *Meditations*, London Dublin 1989, 44.
73. *Idem*, 'Towards a Theology and Philosophy of Unity,' in *The Abba School*, 34.

strongly suggested that relationship is vital to authentic and fulfilled human living. Whether it was the mother and child, the
husband and wife, or the neighbour, in each the relationship
was of paramount importance. To be is to relate: this was the
emerging probability as to the true meaning of human existence.
However, phenomenology welcomes analysis and verification.
Such verification was forthcoming from divine revelation, and
specifically from the mysteries of the Trinity and the cross and
resurrection. In the very relationship of the Covenant, culminating in the 'new and eternal Covenant' of the Word become flesh,
the relationship of God the Holy Trinity to humankind shone
out.

As already noted in the course of chapter nine, St Augustine
drew on the notion of relation in Aristotle in order to speak of
the divine Persons. He saw that relation was no accident of
being in God, for nothing in God is accident. He broke through
to the discovery that 'the meaning of being is self-communicating love'. This is an authentic revolution in our understanding of
being.[74] It is a breakthrough, however, whose potential for
thinking and living has not been exploited.

The flow of thinking in the West during the whole modern
period has indeed set the subject over against being. The snap-
ping of the relation to being is already present in Descartes'
principle. The result is that our concepts are not necessarily con-
nected to what is real. The objects of our thinking are not necessarily real or existent. The outcome has been 'the loss of being'
(Heidegger) and the consequent loss of God. These objects have
been replaced by secularisation, secularism and, most recently,
by post-modernity. It is impossible to understand how God can
fill such a world with himself. 'Thus, for Western people the
world has gradually become empty of meaning. The same goes,
according to some schools of thought, for time and history.'[75] A
cold calculative approach to reality is in place, and substitutes

---

74. Walter Kasper, *The God of Jesus Christ*, 154-6; see n 53.
75. Chiara Lubich, *ibid.*, 35.

for a contemplative one. Thus the beauty, goodness and truth of being or of creation are no longer perceivable.

Here an ontology of relation is both serviceable and effective. As we have seen already, the God of Jesus Christ is the God who engages the creation in all its forsakenness. He took upon himself the condition of creatures separated from the source of being. He entered into what the Book of Qoheleth calls the 'vanity of vanities'. (1:2) He related himself to the 'non-being' of creatures, especially to that of the men and women of our history, and transformed it into himself as that positive 'non-being' which is infinite Love.

II. RECIPROCITY

In an ontology inspired by the Blessed Trinity, reciprocity or mutuality is of the essence. The divine Persons love one another. The New Commandment, as that which is both constitutive of the eschatological mission of the Son and the Holy Spirit, as the very arms of the Father extended over and around the whole human family, is structurally a reciprocity. It has to be such. This necessity is discerned, albeit dimly, in the searching of philosophy all the way from Aristotle's *Nicomachean Ethics* to the research of an Edith Stein. But it is revealed in the mystery of Christ. His very mystery is the mystery of unity, better communion. The hermeneutical key idea to the Second Vatican Council, it leads to a recovery of mutuality. As equal 'I's' of the one human nature, the only appropriate attitude, philosophically speaking, for human beings is the attitude of mutual love. The truth of this insight is empirically verifiable: human beings do in fact flourish in an atmosphere of reciprocal loving.

The life of God has revealed his life as the life of love. And since God is love, he is Trinity. The mission of the Son consists in the bringing of this Trinitarian love to earth. The mission of the Holy Spirit is to ignite this mutual loving in human hearts, enabling human persons actually to live for one another. The Acts portrays the early Jerusalem community as one where there was but 'one mind and one heart'. (Acts 4:32) The result is that the

church is, as the Fathers loved to stress and as the Council grate-
fully remembered, 'a people made one from the unity of the
Father, the Son and the Holy Spirit.'[76] The paschal Christ prays
that the culture of mutuality that he has brought from his homeland in the eternal Trinity will become the culture and life of his
followers on earth: '*Ecclesia enim est mutuo se diligens;*' writes St
Bonaventure in the thirteenth century.[77] Recently a philosopher
could describe 'the church as the created heaven of the Trinity,
while the Trinity is the uncreated heaven of the church.'[78] The
reciprocity of mutual loving brings about Trinitarian relationships, as our next category will show.

III. PERICHORESIS

The effect of loving mutually is that the lovers live in each other.
'As you, Father, are in me and I am in you, may they also be in
us.' (Jn 17:21) In just one sentence, Jesus connects the immanent
and the economic Trinity. The eternal Trinity is a *perichoresis* of
the divine Persons by which they indwell each Other. It becomes
the source of the *perichoresis* of the children of God on earth, for
'We are already the children of God.' (1 Jn 3:2) and are members
of each other, so that 'if one member suffers, all members suffer
with it. If one member is given special honour, all members rejoice with it.' (1 Cor 12:26)

The word, *perichoresis*, was coined by the later Greek Fathers
to describe not only the eternal relationships of the Persons, but
also the unique relationships set up by the trinitarian self-com-
munication to humankind. Initially it served to illumine two
other areas of revealed reality: the relationship between the divine and the human natures in Christ, and the lifestyle of
Christians that would correspond to the existence and the mes-

---

76. St Cyprian, *De oratione dominica*, 23, PL, 4, 553; St Augustine, *Sermo*
71, 20, 33, PL 38, 463f: *Lumen Gentium*, 4.
77. St Bonaventure, *Hexameron* I, 4.
78. Klaus Hemmerle, '*Trinitarische Kirche – Kirche als Communio*' in
Gemeinsam für die Menschheit, Neue Stadt Dokumentation 2, Munchen
1988, 53.

sage of Jesus.[79] 'I am in the Father and the Father is in me.' (Jn 14:10; 10:38b) The origin of the term is quite fascinating. Originally it was the name for a communal dance. The one dances around the other, the other dances around the one, as in an Irish three-hand reel. In that way everything flows in and between the dancers.

Now this is the life that stands out when the dynamic taught and given by Jesus is taken seriously and put into practice. The other person becomes the axis of my life, I am the axis of his life. God is the axis of my life, and – wonderful to tell – I become an axis of his life. Everything unfolds in this 'axial inter-dancing'. The life of the church has to become a great 'School of perichoretic Dancing'. Is not this the central teaching of Pope John Paul II's Apostolic Letter for the third millennium, *Novo Millennio Ineunte*? 'The desire of God for the whole church at the beginning of the third millennium, as well as the desire in the hearts of humankind, is that the church become the home and the school of communion.' (43) There can be no dispensation from this imperative.

This *perichoresis* leads to a radical break with a style of thinking and living that are characterised by individualism and egocentricity. Such individualism and egocentricity are oblivious to the true greatness of our humanity, blind to the gospel of Jesus Christ, and deaf to what the Holy Spirit is saying to the church today. (Rev 2:7) The very core of the gospel need not have been revealed. *Perichoresis*, however, requires a radical shift of perspective. Phrases such as the following capture some of its richness in vivid contemporary idiom, 'Put yourself in the place of the other,' 'Stand in the shoes of the other,' 'Think with the mind of the other and look at things with his eyes.' The communion that Christians are called to be is not a distant goal, but their very identity and the source of the life and the witness they owe the world: 'By this love you have for one another, everyone will know you are my disciples.' (Jn 13:35; 15:12)

There is a particularly poignant illustration of the centrality

79. See n 43.

of such perichoretic categories in a homily of Pope Paul VI on the occasion of a pastoral visit to a Roman parish, 'Remember the burning word of Christ, "They will know you are my disciples if you love one another." When this warmth of sympathy is there, this love; when there is a sympathy among you that is desired as much as felt, and is as spontaneous as it is cultivated, and is joined to an openness of heart and a readiness to witness to Jesus in our midst (because we truly feel ourselves one in him and through him) – only then will we be recognised as his followers, as genuine disciples and believers.'[80]

IV. KENOSIS

The mission of the Son involved a double *kenosis*, that of the incarnation and that of the cross (Phil 2:7-8). This double *kenosis* not only restored our unity with the Father, it also united us all in Jesus and with one another. It was the effective gathering into one of the scattered children of God. (Jn 11:53) Conquered by his love for us, the enfleshed Son becomes what we are, thus completing the incarnation by taking on the human condition, for, as the Fathers loved to repeat, what is not assumed is not redeemed. Such self-emptying, however, cost him the experience of abandonment by the Father on the wood of the cross, 'My God, my God, why have you forsaken me?' (Mk 15:34; Mt 27:46)

This *kenosis* is the means by which the Son united us vertically to his Father and horizontally with one another. The self-emptying Son, in fact, spans the terrible abyss separating sin from the All-holy God, death from life, hell from heaven, and nothing from all. In spanning this abyss, the Son takes on two names that contradict the eternal beauty and goodness of his being: he becomes curse (Gal 3:13) and sin (2 Cor 5:21). The *kenotic* Son thus 'situates' estranged and lost humankind between himself and the Father of mercies. (2 Cor 1:3) By reaching across that terrible divide in re-surrendering himself to the Father (Lk 23:46), he

---

80. Pope Paul VI, text quoted in Chiara Lubich, *Dove due o tre*, Roma 1976, 98-100.

makes every son and daughter of Adam 'vulnerable' to the love
of the Holy Spirit.

This kenotic love of the Son is a true alchemy: the baseness of
our human condition, the sins that mark human history with the
appalling wounds of disunity and mutual hatred leading to
death and destruction, are challenged from within and from beneath. 'Where sin abounded, grace abounded all the more.'
(Rom 5:16) The hope to which Paul in the Letter to the Romans
sings (5:1-5; 8:31-39) has a foundation that amazes. It is the
Christ slain in the place of the sinners. This *kenosis* 'makes possible a discipleship of the cross, a being-in-Christ as kenotic love
for the sinner, which does not reject the sinner or merely tolerate
him, but seeks him out.'[81] Of course, this love will resist sinning
with the sinner, but will prefer to bear the burden of his sin as
one's own.

The great scar of disunity among believers, the division that
'openly contradicts the will of Christ, provides a stumbling
block to the world, and inflicts damage on the most holy cause
of proclaiming the good news to every creature,'[82] now has a
face. It is the face of the kenotic Christ who has become one with
all believers and with all men and women through his love 'to
the end'. The kenotic Christ is therefore the catalyst of unity:
where there is disunity among believers, he inspires many to
labour for unity. For the lost he is hope, for the abandoned he is
company ('I have compassion on the crowd'); for the betrayed
he is fidelity; for the brokenhearted he is consolation (2 Cor 1:1-
3); for the failures he is 'success.'[83] This gives fresh currency to
that great principle worked out by the Fathers in the fourth century, namely: 'Whatever has been taken on has been redeemed.'[84]

81. Matthias Fenski, 'Klaus Hemmerles Verständnis von Einheit –
Wegmarken für eine ökumenische Methodologie,' in Das Prisma, vol 15,
1/2003, 52.
82. Second Vatican Council, Unitatis Redintegratio, The Decree on
Ecumenism, 1.
83. See Chiara Lubich, Il grido, Roma 2000, 43f.
84. See K. Rahner, Misteri della vita di Cristo. Ecce homo!, in Nuovi Saggi,
II, Roma 1968, 173-174.

He is the God who is attracted by the negative, for he is the revelation of a love so great that none greater can be thought. (Eph 3:19)

V. UNITY

In a Trinitarian ontology, there is the blueprint for the resolution of the great question of the One and the Many. It is the question that has engrossed philosophers over the centuries. Blaise Pascal suggested a heuristic of the answer: 'A plurality that cannot be integrated into unity is chaos; unity unrelated to plurality is tyranny.'[85] We looked at this question in chapter one which dealt with divine revelation as it reached its pinnacle in the Word become flesh. There we discovered that Jesus Christ is the key to the answer to this abiding puzzle, since 'He is the point where the one and the many, the universal and the concrete, form a perfect synthesis.'[86] As the eternal Son, he is one, while as the eternal Son made flesh he incorporates into himself the many who are chosen in him 'before the world was made'. (Eph 1:4) As the pre-existing Logos he is universal, but as this Logos become flesh he is utterly particular, being this Jesus of Nazareth. In the words of Irenaeus: 'Christ brought total new-ness by bringing himself.'[87]

Jesus the incarnate Son is the God who harmonises the one and the many. He can do so because he brings with him the life of the eternal One God who is still a communion of Three Persons. Being infinite Love, God is the event of the Trinity. With the Persons indwelling each other perichoretically, God is one. One in being, God is three in Persons.

When this God turns outwards in the 'economic trinity' to Creation he will imprint his image on all his works. Thus all his works will be both one and many. Aquinas answers the question, 'Could God make a better universe?' He answers that 'the perfection of the universe depends essentially on the diversity of

85. Blaise Pascal, *Pensèes*, (ed Chevalier), 809.
86. John O'Donnell, *Hans Urs von Balthasar*, London 1992, 10.
87. St Irenaeus, *Against the Heresies*, IV, 34,1.

natures by which the various levels of goodness are fulfilled, rather than on the multiplying of the individuals within one nature.'[88] This diversity in the created universe may be understood as an expression of the radical difference-in-unity of the Persons of the Trinity.

There is but one Eucharist, but many celebrations of the sacrifice that was offered once for all in a bloody manner. The apostolic structure of the church, to take another example, is one in the papacy, but many in the College of Bishops. The pope can express and speak in the name of the whole church, while the College – 'with the pope and never without that head'[89] – may also speak and act in the name of the whole church. Thus the triune God puts his fingerprints as it were on the hierarchy of the church.

The new Paradigm for Thinking: Loving

Divine revelation 'opens up vistas closed to human reason.'[90] In a particular way, revelation shows the human family being lifted up into a new milieu, and 'having access to the Father through the Son in the Holy Spirit,' as the *Constitution on Divine Revelation* stresses. The crucified and glorified Christ now draws all men and women with him towards the Father in the power of the Holy Spirit. (Jn 12:32) The economic Trinity reveals and communicates the immanent Trinity to humankind and creation. (1 Jn 1:1-4; Col 3:1-3) The result is that the destination of Creation is nothing less than that of being lifted up into the movement of the Trinitarian life. The place where this begins to happen is the church, for 'The church is a people made one from the unity of the Father, the Son and the Holy Spirit.' As the mystery of Christ spreading out in space and time, the church is the sacrament of unity of the whole human family with God the Holy Trinity and

---

88. St Thomas, *In Sententias*, I, 44.1.2, quoted in Norman Kretzmann, *The Metaphysics of Creation: Aquinas' Natural Theology in* Summa contra Gentiles, II, Oxford 1999, 224, n.106.
89. *Lumen Gentium*, Nota Praevia.
90. *Gaudium et Spes*, 24.

with one another, as the *Constitution on the Church* emphasises.[91]

The unity of the human family 'in the beginning' provides the presupposition and foundation for this unity. So much is this the case that the Fathers always set out from the unity of humankind before they consider the many individuals composing it. For example, Gregory of Nyssa dared to say that, according to scripture, it would be just as shocking to speak of the many making up humankind as to speak of three Gods in the Trinity![92] Vatican II reiterates the same anthropology: 'In the beginning God made human nature one.'[93] Through sin an atomisation of humankind began. The person and the message and the legacy of Jesus Christ is the overcoming of this atomisation. Christ has inserted a new dynamic into history. It is the dynamic of a 'passover' from the sin-driven atomisation of humankind into separated and clashing individuals and towards reunification with Jesus Christ and, through him, in the communion of the Blessed Trinity. The life of the church can only be that of love, and not any love, but precisely the interpersonal love of the Trinity. 'Love one another *as* I have loved you.' 'May they be one in us, *as* you are in me and I am in you.' The culture of this New People has to be the culture of mutual loving.

Authentic Christian praxis requires this life of *agape*. Such praxis, however, must then generate a new style of thinking and acting in order to inspire and ensoul a renewed Christian culture. In this way, the dramatic hiatus of faith and culture, identified by Pope Paul VI as the most dramatic development of our times,[94] can become the occasion of breakthrough to a new culture with a new style of thinking. This would then see the dawning of a new art, economics, politics, communications media,

---

91. *Lumen Gentium*, 1; see Joseph Ratzinger, 'The Church as the Sacrament of Salvation' in *Principles of Catholic Theology*, San Francisco 1987, 44-55.

92. St Gregory of Nyssa, *De hominis opificio*, ch. 15: PG, 44, 185 B – D; see Henri de Lubac, *Catholicism*, London 1950, especially chapter I, 'Dogma', 1-13.

93. *Lumen Gentium*, 13.

94. Pope Paul VI, Apostolic Letter *Evangelii Nuntiandi*, 20.

health and education practice. It is here that a trinitarian ontology comes strongly into view since it indicates the necessary
new 'thinking-style' appropriate to our circumstances and con-
sonant with 'the signs of our times'. This thinking-style would
include the elements of the Trinitarian ontology outlined in our
previous section.

In the revelation of the Trinity, Christ is the Word and expression of the Father, and the Holy Spirit is the expression of
Christ. What is the expression of the human person? It must be
that of love. For just as a divine Person is precisely by not being,
out of love, the human person is when he lives by the same logic
and is a nothingness of love towards God and his sisters and
brothers. 'Anyone who loses his life for my sake, and for the
sake of the gospel, will save it.' (Mk 8:35)

Does this not lead towards another kind of rationality, a
rationality already strongly insinuated in trinitarian ontology? It
is easy to perceive the principle that true rationality consists in
loving as emerges in the fact of Jesus crucified and forsaken.
This is the strong contention of Paul: in his vehement debate
with the Corinthian community as to the nature of true philosophy and the true locus of wisdom, he proposes the crucified
Christ. In its wisdom, the world did not recognise 'the Lord of
glory' and so rejected 'the word of the cross'. (1 Cor 1:18) For
Paul, though, the logic of the cross is the most divine *and* the
most human logic. The deepest rationality is the rationality implicit in the deepest love, the love that 'no eye has seen, nor ear
heard, the heart of man ever imagined.' (1 Cor 2:8)[95]

Now the crucified Christ reveals the love 'that is beyond all
knowing'. (Eph 3:19) Concretely this happened in his forsakenness on the wood of the cross when he cried out in abandonment
to the God who did not reply. 'The eternal Word made flesh asks
why? In this question there is a declaration: the failure of the

---

95. Few people have seen this so clearly as Fyodor Dostoyevsky who in
The Idiot attempts to 'expound the Christian theme of the fool with such
discretion and at the same time such precision that he remains its master,' Hans Urs von Balthasar, *The Glory of the Lord*, V, 201.

Word. Precisely the Word who ought to explain and interpret has to ask. He asks, "why?" He does not know and does not understand. This is the failure of the Word. However, St John declares that at the very summit of this abandonment, the Word made man "hands over the Spirit".[96] Now the Spirit is communion, being the love that unites the Father and the Son, and that overflows on to humankind in this supreme 'hour' of the Father's love (Rom 8:32) as well as of the Son's love 'for us' (Gal 2:20) and for one another. He is the Spirit whose fruitfulness will be manifest at Pentecost, forming and honing the church as a People made 'one in mind and heart'. (Acts 4:32) It was this unity-communion that enabled the first Jerusalem community to 'say' and to 'tell' the gospel by first being the gospel. As the early chapters of Acts love to repeat, they were 'the followers of the Way' before everything else, the name 'Christian' being applied only later. (Acts 11:26)

The time has come for a similar communion, for this is the only way to tell the same good news of the Christ who remains 'the same yesterday, today and forever'. (Heb 13:8) The movement of history has brought us to this point. That is why Pope John Paul II writes in *Novo Millennio Ineunte* that 'to make the church the home and the school of communion ... is the great challenge facing us in the millennium which is now beginning, if we wish to be faithful to God's plan and respond to the world's deepest needs.' (43)

A word of explanation is in order. Our world is, or rather has been, a world of the word and the concept. From the Greek discovery of *logos* as a prime constituent of human being all the way to the modern period, the single concept has been the central and abiding object of all human thinking, the goal of art, the guiding principle in human action. In a word, *logos* was the hallmark of rationality. In recent times, however, the culture of *logos* has run into bad times. We see the crisis most clearly perhaps in the phenomenon of deconstruction, which suspects the Word of

---

96. Giuseppe Zanghí, *Gen's Rivista di vita ecclesiale*, XXXII 6 (2002), '*L'alba di un mondo diverso,*' 180.

meaninglessness, and subjects the greatest expressions of the word to a critique that threatens to empty them of the very substance intended by their authors. An Italian thinker describes the scenario in these terms: '[There is] the proliferation of words, the disorientation of thought, the disappearance of the philosopher, the person of wisdom; the silence of art washed out by the domination of the word-concept; the advent of "collective" thinking required by technology and the media but which risks cancelling the unique quality of the individual and the initial wonder.'[97]

Each of us, as a word spoken and chosen eternally in the eternal consubstantial Word of the Father, is called to be a nothingness of love in order to let the eternal Word speak himself fully against that background, like a painting set against its background. That Word speaks himself fully only when we live what is deepest in his heart, namely, the love that he calls both 'his' and 'new', the New Commandment. We have just seen the elements emerging from this new commandment. This, in fact, is the new culture: not in the first instance a library of books, but living persons united in the sweet bonds of love. 'Look how these Christians love one another, and are willing to die for each other.'[98]

Human language operates on the basis of the sentence which requires a subject, a verb and normally some words. If I should use the words 'We', 'ship', 'ocean' without a verb, I would make no sense whatsoever. However, if I should say, 'We see a ship on the ocean', the verb gives meaning to everything. Here the verb rescues all the substantives from meaninglessness. The verb is now the 'new substantive,' as we have already seen in this chapter. For our part, each of us is a 'word' created in the Word and re-created in the Word made flesh. However, when we encounter as 'words' in Jesus we remain without sense and without meaning until, and only if, we are linked by loving, indeed,

---

97. *Idem, 'Il pensare come amore. Verso un nuovo paradigma culturale'* in *Nuova Umanità*, XXIV, 1(2003), 14-15.
98. Tertullian, *Apologeticum*, 39, 7: CSEL 69.

concrete loving. Only the verb 'loving' gives meaning to our gathering. 'By this all will know you are my disciples, if you love one another.' (Jn 13:35) It is no accident that Jesus never says this of anything else. A Trinitarian ontology grounds and guides the new paradigm for thinking in its manifold expressions.

Conclusion

Ontology as the science of being has fallen on difficult times. The unfolding of Western culture, as well as the plenitude of goods and technical benefits flowing from science and technology, conspired against its flourishing. The light of being has waned, and the colours of being, what the tradition calls the 'transcendentals,' have gone below the horizon. Patrick Kavanagh could invite his contemporaries to 'see a star-lovely art in every sod,'[99] since Christ had bathed all of creation in his re-creating eternal beauty. However, the conspiracy of positivism has reached the point of making us forget the wonder that 'there is something and not simply nothing' (Leibniz) as the first of all wonders. The situation has been further aggravated by the failure of Christians to think out fully the ontological equivalent of divine revelation and thus to impact and create a culture. Still, this historical deficit has been allowed by the Lord of History for a good purpose: perhaps only now is 'the distinctively Catholic' (Heinrich Schlier) of divine revelation in a position to propose a truly Paschal and Trinitarian ontology. Since Being is love, that ontology will have categories that transform the inherited categories of substance and accident by forging new ones. The latter will open up a world of beauty requiring a new onto-logic of thinking, of loving and, above all, of doing.

---

99. Parick Kavanagh, *The Complete Poems*, New York and Newbridge 1972, 'Ploughman', 2.

Index of Names